EARTHMAKER

▲▲▲▲▲▲▲▲▲▲▲▲

EARTHMAKER

▼▼▼▼▼▼▼▼▼▼▼

TRIBAL STORIES FROM
NATIVE
NORTH AMERICA

JAY MILLER, PH.D.

A PERIGEE BOOK

To my ancestors,
who told great stories.

Perigee Books
are published by
The Putnam Publishing Group
200 Madison Avenue
New York, NY 10016

Library of Congress Cataloging-in-Publication Data

Earthmaker: tribal stories from native North America / [compiled by]
Jay Miller.
p. cm.
Includes bibliographical references and index.
ISBN 0-399-51779-0
1. Indians of North America—Legends. 2. Indians of North
America—Religion and mythology. I. Miller, Jay.
E98.F6E13 1992   92-8581   CIP
398.2'08997—dc20

Cover design by Mike McIver
Cover photo © by H. Armstrong Roberts, Inc.

Printed in the United States of America
1 2 3 4 5 6 7 8 9 10

This book is printed on acid-free paper.
∞

CONTENTS

FOREWORD
▼▼▼▼▼▼

The natives of the Americas, after centuries of life on their own, suffered an invasion from Europe and Africa. As the original people of this "New World" they were subjected to diseases, missions, foreign laws and treaties, and schools. Yet they survived. A major factor in their survival was the vitality of their traditions, sprung from American soil and nourished despite change, stress, and conflict.

Among the most successful of antidotes to European attempts at domination has been the Native ability to laugh and love. Key expressions of these feelings are stories such as the ones that appear between the covers of this book. Natives told of their joys and sorrows, their hopes and fears, and their plans and misadventures in stories that reflected the times and places of their telling.

These stories were best expressed in the thousands of languages spoken in North America. As people learned to use Spanish, French, or English, however, these stories were transposed into these new languages. While some nuances and subtleties were lost in the process, the import of the story remained. In both instances, the who, what, when, where, why, and the way it was told colored the version that was given.

The stories collected and retold here were all based in a Native language, but translated into English. They are Native stories re-phrased into the conversational style so characteristic of Native tellings. Details and motivations have been supplied because these were usually left for the audience to fill in. Characters, situations, and circumstances were so well known to all that they could be left unstated. Here they have been added to increase understanding and appreciation.

Most Americans have only a vague knowledge that Native Americans and tribes continue to live on. Often, their notions are clouded with romantic misunderstandings or projections about ecological harmony, gender equality, and a profound spirituality, which is lacking in their modern world. There are no stories of lovers' leaps, great battles, or faithful Indian companions here. Every selection expresses issues with cultural significance to the people involved. While it is very true that Natives lead more integrated and satisfying lives than most urbanites, this has to do with a sense of their own place in an on-going tradition.

Tribal members know who they are because they know the stories of their people, their home, and their environment. Although missionaries and schools have tried to sever these bonds, they have persisted. Children and adults were wounded in fighting against this domination, but communities survived. Elders cherished the stories and passed them on to guarantee their survival.

Today, television is more a threat to stories and traditions than missionaries and teachers ever were. The media are insidious because generalized and commercialized cartoons replace ancient trickers. Extra efforts must be made at home and in school to have these stories continue. Books now have their place as repositories of a record. They are not as good as hearing and seeing the stories told, but they help.

As times change, so do the stories. Coyote is now as likely to run afoul of a car as he did of a bison in the old days. That is the nature of a coyote living today. Yet that same coyote might also take hearers back to a time of leather clothing and mat lodges when stone tools helped with the work.

The stories collected here are intended to tell of the old time, before Europeans and Africans came in huge numbers and before changes were forced on the Americas. They are written in a slightly more formal style of speaking because they represent the literature of Native America. They are based on widespread and deeply rooted versions well reported in a Native language as well as in English translation.

They tell of times and places that still exist in America, ready to be savored by other people sharing the same continent without knowing that it is a holy land. It was formed by divine forces in the beginning, shaped and adjusted early on, and prepared for the eventual arrival of humans, the last of whom came back from Europe after they had been sent there.

Every tribe has its own coherent traditions explained within its local context. These are best left with the people themselves. By sampling a range of these traditions, however, we can sense the commonalities which make American traditions distinctive among world civilizations.

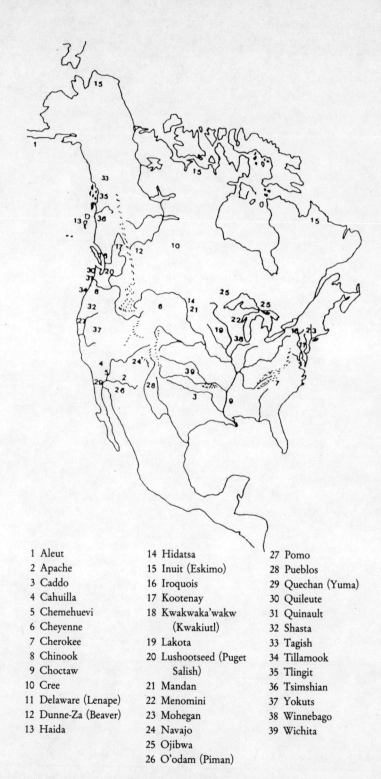

1 Aleut
2 Apache
3 Caddo
4 Cahuilla
5 Chemehuevi
6 Cheyenne
7 Cherokee
8 Chinook
9 Choctaw
10 Cree
11 Delaware (Lenape)
12 Dunne-Za (Beaver)
13 Haida

14 Hidatsa
15 Inuit (Eskimo)
16 Iroquois
17 Kootenay
18 Kwakwaka'wakw
   (Kwakiutl)
19 Lakota
20 Lushootseed (Puget
   Salish)
21 Mandan
22 Menomini
23 Mohegan
24 Navajo
25 Ojibwa
26 O'odam (Piman)

27 Pomo
28 Pueblos
29 Quechan (Yuma)
30 Quileute
31 Quinault
32 Shasta
33 Tagish
34 Tillamook
35 Tlingit
36 Tsimshian
37 Yokuts
38 Winnebago
39 Wichita

INTRODUCTION
▼▼▼▼▼▼

Stories are the stuff of life throughout the Americas. They occur everywhere. They are the glue holding everything together. Nothing of importance happens that does not involve people telling tales. They bring people together. At gatherings like feasts, weddings, and funerals, much time is devoted to listening while someone recites a favorite tale known to all.

Familiar characters doing familiar things provide assurance to people in the midst of change and flux. Non-Indian children and adults may have their best-loved stories, but these do not compare to Native ones. For non-Indians they are pastimes or diversions. For Native Americans they are part of the fabric of life. They uphold traditions and beliefs. They are not about any place or any time, they are about this hill over there or that time when people still hunted with bows and arrows.

They are about a world of actions, of places, of people, and of wonders. There is not a lot of explanation. No Native American needs it. Instead, there is a sense of being rooted in ancient and comfortable surroundings. Motivations are not spelled out. People understand them because they still occur all around them. Events are lived out today as they have always been since their first mention in a story. Someone is hurt or killed, revenge is expected. Food appears in plenty, a feast will be held and people will share. A person thinks only of her or himself, sorcery will happen. A man or woman is called handsome, a marriage or dalliance will delight the audience. If these expectations do not occur, then a twist will complicate the plot and the audience will be in suspense until things turn out right.

The precise qualities of these actions will depend on where they are happening. North America is a big place, filled with a rich and complex diversity in which Natives still delight. Differences are good, even beneficial. Things should not be the same. Variety is more than the spice of life, it is life itself. This is a teaching lost to the modern world.

Everyone is not the same, either in time or in space. From the beginning, people did not even have a set form. The world was inchoate, exaggerated, and undifferentiated in terms of current categories and forms. Time had no chronology attached to it. The world of mythic epic and the world of the present are forever bound together because events mentioned in myths permanently altered things in ways that account for existing features.

The first beings, often called the Animal People, were simultaneously spirits, species, and shimmering shapes. They had neither form nor substance. They glowed like mirages or illusions. Their colors, if not drab, were iridescent, indeterminate in hue or intensity. These were the prototypes for life forms. Only the supernaturals have retained these characteristics into the present.

With the end of the Epic Age, the onset of graduated time and history, people had to choose or be forced to take permanent forms, at least on the outside. Animal People transformed in many ways. Some did indeed become animals, and some became plants, or bugs, or monsters. Others became rocks, trees, snow, wind, rain, or any of a multitude of features and factors playing a part in the modern world.

And so humans believe. These are not entertainments or amusements, although they have these aspects. They are articles of belief. They locate tribes in time and in space. They establish rituals, customs, and commandments. Things are done now or happen at times because of what occurred in the storied past.

Exactly what happens and when depends on features of culture and environment. These vary across North America in regular ways. They are factors of landscapes and of traditions, of accident and of history.

From the beginning, Native peoples could look at their surroundings and know that they had had no other. They were literally and figuratively rooted in the land. Their world was created there, as were all of their ancestors. Even if they had moved into a new area, they could always point to where they had started and could walk back to it. They knew the beginning and ending of their own lives and those of everyone else who had been or would be important to them.

Those from Europe, with its waves of migrant hordes and its frequent dislocations, could neither understand nor appreciate this profound sense of place, of being precisely located in a world long sanctified by the actions and intentions of your own remote past.

When Native stories are told to American audiences, this sense of place is usually ignored and modern hearers do not understand the profundity of this belief. When stories are published, their exact locale is left unspecified. That is as it should be. To localize these stories is to make them Native American, to place them within a religious context. To make them public is to enrich them, but, at the same time, to remove them from Native contexts and traditions.

As often as not, when a Native storyteller recounts a legend to his or her own people, they all share a vivid image of the terrain being crossed, the characters in action, and the lasting effects of the events. Unfortunately, only the oldest of the audience will be able to remember the landscape as it was in nature. Younger members will have to be reminded that where the shopping center is now was where Grandmother Toad had her house, or where the fight between the brothers occurred is now an open pit mine.

It is a tribute to the Native sense of place that people can still look at a locale and see it as their ancestors did. They can filter out the filth and wish for things as they were. They can still believe in a world although its physical form has been changed forever. With the Black Hills of South Dakota, devastated by mining and development, Lakota people continue to emphasize their sacred dimensions rather than their scars.

People became members of tribes and natives of the Americas on this continent. It was from this soil and space that they developed a separate identity. America was their only home. Yet it was from Asia that the human ancestors of these people came. They came as hunters and harvesters crossing the grassy plain created when water from the seas became frozen as glaciers.

They came with stories. They came with skills. In America, they learned to listen to the spirits of the many places where power could be collected and passed on. They became Americans by becoming sensitive to their abode. That made it their own and themselves a part of it.

They came in small bands of close and caring families. They respected age and wisdom. They acquired more feeling for these as they settled. Filling both North and South America with a sparse population, they prospered. Some specialized. From the beginning, there were those who hunted and those who harvested. Usually, the men would hunt and the women would harvest. Together, couples learned to tend their landscape, seeking to caress it during their lives. They coaxed and they nourished, but they did not intrude in any major earth-shaking ways. When mounds were built or hillsides terraced, people were following the directives of spirits familiar with the best uses of those terrains.

Members of these bands and tribes tended wild foods such as plants, trees, vines, and berries. Every year, they burned over large sections of land to encourage fresh growth and unobstructed passage. Some tended seafoods and shores, building huge traps to impound live fish during low tides. Others gave their attention to herds of animals like mammoths and bison. In the North, people cared for a variety of animals who lived apart, such as moose. Humans and animals kept track of each other and lived off their kills. Both died, but with mutual respect.

In time, the specialized tending of plants developed into a more intensive tilling of the soil. New species were fostered, encouraged by the human hand. The spirits of particular species appeared in visions and in stories to explain what people needed to do. Sunflowers, amaranth, sunroot, and various local seeds began the process of specialization, while corn, beans, squash, manioc, and potatoes brought it to fruition.

All of these interactions were recorded in stories, each of them making clear that underneath the outer forms of these species there was an essential human form with arms, legs, and hands. This common, underlying humanity provided the basis for a system of beliefs shared across the diverse regions of the Americas.

Starting with the hunting and harvesting pattern of the migrants from Asia, a variety of adaptations were developed by Native Americans as they made the continent their own.

These "culture areas" have come to be defined in terms of their staple foods, housing styles, family arrangements, and, particularly, organizing rituals.

For Tenders, these regions, from north to south, are the Arctic, Subarctic, Northwest Coast, California, and Intermontane.

Initially the last haven of the big game hunting tradition, interacting with enormous herds of bison, the Plains added farming as people settled in sheltered river valleys. With the reintroduction of the horse into the Americas by Spanish explorers, the Plains again emphasized hunting as it became populated by tribes from many other regions who came to live with the bison herds.

For the Tillers, the Southwest and East relied on farming, located at the frontiers of Mexican empires and religious movements. The economies of the valley of Mexico were fueled by trade goods and foodstuffs from the far-flung reaches of the Americas.

As an introduction to North America, each of these culture areas will be considered in turn to provide a context for appreciating the variety of stories throughout the continent.

ARCTIC

While much of the Arctic year consists of cold, white winters, there are a few months of long days and wet terrain. Almost unique on the earth, its Inuit (Eskimo) inhabitants stretch along a coastal zone and share a similar appearance, language, culture, and environment. This is not often the case because looks, language, and locale do not often coincide.

Tundra is the predominant landform, covered with ice fields all winter long. With little vegetation, hunting was the basis for life. Living on the land are musk-ox, caribou, fox, bear, and wolf, along with hare, marmots, and lemmings. Birds include ptarmigan, owl, plover, and seagull. Coastal rivers abound with fish, while the ocean has seals, whales, walrus, and sea lions.

Among the strongest Inuit taboos is the prohibition on mixing food from the sea with that from the land. Seal meat must be served separately from caribou. Winter houses were made of sod, stone, and timbers, while camping used tents and igloos.

Men and women had separate but equal responsibilities. Only married couples could survive. Men did the hunting, while women processed and cooked the food that fed the family. Men used kayaks, while the umiaks that moved families and household gear were associated with women. In Alaska, villages also had a separate men's house.

Usually, a house was occupied by a married couple and their children, together with a grandparent or other stray relative. A superb hunter or shaman might have more than one wife, but this was rare. Every house had a men's and a women's domain. Usually, the hard floor, used as a work surface, and the cold outer storage compartment belonged to men, while the fur-covered sleeping platform where the family spent the day and slept at night belonged to the women. The wife was especially equated with the soapstone lamp that lit and warmed the house, using oil rendered from animals killed by her husband.

During seasons of plenty, families might gather together to form kindreds or "bands," but these lasted only a few days until provisions ran low. Leaders emerged only long enough to coordinate a particular task, such as net fishing or caribou hunting, and then submerged back into the crowd. While respected at all times, these men only led during situations when everyone needed to work together.

Community sentiments were expressed through a series of formal arrangements confirmed by the brief exchange of wives, good-natured insults, trade goods, names, and hunting partnerships. People conformed to public expectations through the application of subtle pressures expressed by means of ridicule, songs, and snide remarks. If there was no improvement, slugging contests might be tried, to be followed by ostracism, which was tantamount to death, or, in the worst of antisocial behavior, sanctioned murder.

Shamans were individuals, often men but sometimes women, who had special relationships with the supernatural. Often, certain families produced effective shamans generation after generation. Shamans cured both the illness of a person and the social ills of the community.

In the most dramatic of all cures, a shaman mystically journeyed to the ocean bottom to comb tangles out of the hair of Sedna, the woman in charge of all the animals. Taboo violations, abuse of animals, and ill-will by humans caused these tangles, and the shaman undertook to soothe Sedna so she would send the animals back to the hunters. He could only apply the comb to Sedna after someone had confessed to the breaches that caused these problems. With this personal confession came absolution for the entire community.

The major public ritual came at midwinter when people gathered to feast on stored and frozen foods, engage in games, and learn from their stories. In Alaskan men's houses, elaborate mask enactments were held.

SUBARCTIC

Evergreens such as pine, spruce, hemlock, and fir dominate the forests that cover this huge area. Along broad streams where moose thrive are willow, tamarack, birch, alder, and poplar. Other inhabitants are wolf, lynx, wolverine, bear, and caribou, along with the snowshoe rabbit, martin, and great horned owl. In high alpine meadows lives the pika, a rabbit relative who sun dries and stores grass and twigs for winter feeding.

Regional staples include caribou, along with salmon in the west, wild rice in the Great Lakes, and moose and deer in the east.

Married couples formed the basic unit of every community. Men engaged in hunting, trapping, and tool making. Women did the cleaning and storing of fish and game, tended the household, and raised the children. Fishing provided an opportunity for men and women to work together, otherwise the genders worked apart. Families generally lived together under the influence of a parent or older sibling. Leadership depended on the task at hand, but the pool of respected elders who might serve as leader consisted of those individuals known for their hunting success, good character, sensible decisions, spirit allies, and generosity. Individuals communicated with their spirit partners via dreams, which provided help or warnings about upcoming activities. In all situations, elders led by example, never by command.

When trading posts and the fur trade came to the north, larger groupings into bands and tribes were encouraged. People along the same drainage often cooperated so that some could hunt for food while others trapped furs. It was difficult to do both and survive.

Only shamans had a recognized position in the community. He or she healed the sick, prayed for successful hunts, and directed puberty ceremonies for girls on the verge of womanhood. The health, number, and stability of their own families served as testimony for their abilities.

Tribes often traced the origin of the world to an Earth Diver. Among the Beaver or Dunne-za tribe, Muskrat retrieved the dirt that became the earth, while Swan had the more prophetic role of establishing the cultural rules and social conventions. Among his greatest contributions was stealing fire for humans. Throughout the western section, the Give Away was the communal ceremony, much like the Potlatch of the Northwest Coast. Families celebrated their own prestige and gained honor by being generous to others.

Among Great Lakes tribes, the Midewiwin or Grand Medicine Lodge had the most distinctive rituals in the region. Emphasizing a belief in rebirth, initiates were symbolically killed and revived in order to achieve membership. After physical death, members were inducted into a ghost lodge.

In the west, the Shaking Tent provided a means for special shamans to hold a seance in which members of the audience outside the conical tent could ask questions and receive a reply from visiting spirits, particularly Turtle and Owl. As each spirit entered the tent, it shook violently, even though no one could make it budge before the start of the ritual.

NORTHWEST COAST

Rain and mountains characterize this region, thickly covered by evergreen forests and drained by many waterways. Red cedar was a particular gift of the Creator, providing the straight-grained planks that became the sides of houses, and the logs that were used to form molded canoes, bentwood boxes, and tools of local tribes. Travel was by water because the dense undergrowth of thickets and brambles made land routes few and far between, except along riverbanks.

Salmon was the staple, gathered by men and women during huge runs during the spring and summer months. Candlefish in the north and acorns in the south augmented the diet. Food grew in abundance and variety, taken by means of an elaborate technology. Men were concerned with animals and fish, while women devoted considerable time to plant foods, from the fresh greens of spring to the berries and nuts of autumn.

Winter towns included a row of big plank houses facing the beach, each house inhabited by related families. In the north, kinship was traced through women of various clans; in the central zone, it was traced through both parents, while in the south, the father's side was given more emphasis. Northern towns were also divided into halves, variously Orca and Raven or Eagle and Raven, which included different clans.

A "house" was the dwelling place of three ranks of people. At the rear of the house, beside its sacred treasures of masks, costumes, and carvings, lived the nobles who owned the house. The eldest man was the leader of the household, but his wife (in the middle) or sister (in the north) provided links among the members. Along the sides were families of commoners who attached themselves to the house as kin or workers. Beside the door were slaves, taken in war or the children of such captives, whose lives belonged to their owner, along with all of their labor.

Families kept their own fires along the sides of the house where they lived. In the middle, however, was a large hearth used to cook meals for the noble owners or for guests attending a celebration. Houses owned stories, sacred histories, naming the people, places, and resources claimed by ancestors. Some of these house histories can be related to regional patterns in existence for over two thousand years. These involved the location of fishing, berry-ing, seaweeding, and hunting sites claimed by a specific house. Most stories in the Northwest, therefore, are owned and copyrighted by households. Only a few are phrased in such general terms that they were widely known and used to teach a moral.

The major event throughout this region was the Potlatch, an elaborate feast when a noble family dramatized their clan crests and treasures (via songs, dances, masks, effigies, and natural rarities) inside of a house filled with invited guests. In return for witnessing and validating the copyrights of the nobles and the transmissions to their children, guests received abundant food and gifts. Later, guests would host their own Potlatch and reciprocate the hospitality of their former hosts.

Raven, the being who transformed the world, hosted the first Potlatch before he ended the mythic age prior to the arrival of humans. Not surprisingly, Raven is an important figure of legend on both sides of the Pacific, not just the North American one but the Asian side as well.

After closely studying the collection called *Tsimshian Mythology* (1916)—assembled by Henry Tate, a commoner, and William Bey-non, a chief—Franz Boas, the great scholar of this area, was able to describe how the Tsimshian viewed their world in traditional times.

Accordingly, the earth was a flat disk supported on a pole resting on the chest of Am'ala, a spirit who had replaced a previous supernatural Atlas. In the mythic age, all of the future people and animals lived together at Prairie Town on the upper Skeena River. After a flood, everyone left Prairie Town and settled in separate towns or houses on the earth. Animals retained their human forms only within their own settlements.

When a male bear had his fishing line break or a female bear had her tumpline snap, it meant that they had been killed by a human hunter. In a few days, he or she would return to Bear Town provided that they had been treated with proper ritual by the hunter and his kin.

On the edge of the earth, Pestilence Chief, his daughter, and maimed people lived together. The ocean surrounded the earth and in it lived fish and sea mammals. Orcas were divided into the same four units (semi-moieties or phratries composed of clusters of clans) as the Tsimshian themselves and displayed their crest membership by the form of their dorsal fins. Across the ocean were different worlds inhabited by dwarfs, birds, ghosts, and salmon.

In the Salmon Country, each species had its own town, with the Spring Salmon furthest away and the Silver, Steelhead, Humpback, Coho, and Trout successively closer to the ocean and the earth.

The Spring Salmon sent scouts up the Skeena River to see if what they called their salmon were spawning. With a favorable report, the Springs started out announcing the good news to the other Salmon towns as they passed them. The Silvers, Humpbacks, and Dogs announced that they would follow shortly; the Cohos that they would wait until fall; the Trout asked to accompany the Springs; and these two together continued on to meet the Steelhead who were already returning from the Skeena. What the Salmon called their salmon, humans called cottonwood leaves which had fallen into the river.

Spanning this terrestrial realm was the Sky World, from which various supernaturals, generally called "shining youths," descended to earth during four flashes of lightning and four claps of thunder in order to help or to marry a mortal.

Such a being was Raven, who arrived as a shining youth and became a voracious glutton who changed the world forever through his selfishness and greediness, benefitting people only inadvertently, incidentally, or accidentally.

Raven's wide appeal derives from the complexity of his character, which allowed an audience to ponder many possibilities ranging from identity to catharsis. Among his important characteristics were superhuman powers and abilities, social license, and entertaining incongruities. Yet he shaped the larger distinctions of the modern world by skill, cunning, and incredible feats of wonder and stupidity.

Humans can identify with his omnipotence and craftiness, while holding up his disgusting activities to scorn. As a bumbling host, an amorous interloper, or a devious glutton, he provided an abundance of negative examples. Like Raven, a narrator had complete license to say the unsayable, plot the unthinkable, exalt the lowly, and defame the mighty. This was the cathartic appeal of Raven.

Further, Raven created some delightful paradoxes, as when he convinced Bear that a stone had insulted it, or when Raven was swallowed by a whale and lived inside it by stripping off meat and cooking it.

The Raven cycle is remarkably open-ended, as alive today as ever. Louis Shotridge, a Tlingit, remarked that serious or transforming episodes should occur in a logical order, while the humorous or trickster incidents might occur anywhere that a narrator felt his audience would appreciate them.

Viola Garfield, another important scholar of the region, made the point that Raven's own life cycle established a chronology for the entire series of stories.

In brief, Raven was born in the sky of an incestuous or an unfaithful mother. He descended to earth as a shining youth, but became humanized both by a ritual adoption as well as by eating scabs. The overall effect of this was to make him voracious, setting the motivation for his subsequent adventures. Oblivious to humans, his greed led him to differentiate the world by tricking various owners into releasing the Sun, Moon, and Stars; Fresh Water, Candlefish, the Tides, Fair Weather, Fire, Death, Salmon, and Land. He gave many animals their present attributes, painting colors on birds and cutting out the tongue of Cormorant. In still other episodes, Raven was humiliated, teased, and maligned. Always, he sought food. Finally, Raven moved out to sea, invited the sea monsters to the first Potlatch, feasted and entertained them, and either received their promise not to harm humans or turned them and himself into stone.

After the time of Raven came a host of changers, shapers, or transformers. The gross differentiations of Raven's world became the backdrop for details and particulars added by these men. While Raven usually worked alone, transformers came in teams, although only the most prominent member was named.

Most shapers came from elsewhere. Some simply appeared on earth; others descended from the sky, or were born as the offspring of marriages between animals and humans. Transformer cycles ranged from the Straits of Georgia to the Oregon coast, featuring Mink toward the north and Bluejay toward the south, both renowned for their amorous adventures and improprieties.

Shapers created much of the contemporary landscape, set the ancestry of names and privileges, invented useful tools, and gave animals their present forms and attributes. For example, when transformers met people sharpening weapons to commit murder, they used the very same weapons to change these people into animals. Thus, a spear became the tail of mink or otter, while a knife or paddle formed that of beaver.

Eventually, transformers went away, other replacement teams no longer arrived, or, according to the Quinault and Quileute, shapers turned to stone near the mouth of the Columbia River after they had created various tribes from wolves or dogs, made mouths with the slash of a knife, or set certain people upright who used to walk on their hands and carry things with their feet.

Among tales that thrive to this day along the North Pacific are fearful accounts that deal with the dangers of the sea and of the impenetrable forest bramble. Monsters still live in these remote places. These range from Land Otter People of the north to the Sasquatch or Wild Man of the south. For the Tlingit, Haida, and Tsimshian, Land Otter Men still capture drowned humans and change them into Land Otters with human fingernails. Land Otters have the ability to mimic the appearance of someone, often a sweetheart, that a human alone in the woods is thinking about or longing for.

The Kwakwaka'wakw (Kwakiutl) recognized a Wild Man (Bukwas), who captured people by offering them food. Approaching someone stranded on a beach or near freezing, Bukwas stood in the bow of a canoe whose crew was Land Otters who looked like the victim's relatives, minks who acted as paddles, and a skate who was the canoe itself. The Fraser River Salish have a similar being called Sasquatch, who stole women and food.

Copper, dentalia or tusk shells, and abalone retain their great value along the entire coast. Among northern tribes, spirits able to confer treasures included a giant Beaver with copper eyes, claws, ears, and teeth.

According to the Tagish of the Yukon, the famous Klondike Gold Rush of 1898 started with an Indian's encounter with Wealth Woman, who had long fingernails and wore martin skins, dentalia, and copper. Traditionally, her nails were also copper, but since the Rush, she has been described as having gold fingernails.

CALIFORNIA

Ruggedly mountainous, divided into many steep valleys, California was covered with oak forests populated by grizzly bears, mule deer, and a variety of rodents, quails, and reptiles.

Acorns were the staple, treated by complicated leaching to remove toxins before they could be cooked and eaten. Salmon, seals, insects, shellfish, and many plant foods filled the diet.

More different languages were spoken in aboriginal California than anywhere else on the continent, their variety encouraged by the ruggedness of the terrain.

Married couples lived in their own houses with their children and other unattached relatives. These houses clustered in small villages. Houses in the north were made of wooden planks, while those in the south were built of branches and fibers. Villages in the north also had men's houses used for rituals, club activities, and saunas.

Men did the hunting and women the gathering. The genders cooperated during the harvest of acorns, which women then hulled, ground, leached, and stored as meal. Women also made some of the finest baskets known to the world.

In the south, people belonged to clans inherited through the father and moieties or halves, called Coyote and Wildcat, traced through the mother. In general, the female was regarded as the generalized aspect of life, while the male was the specialized. The moieties were therefore open categories organizing each community, while the paternal clans were finely graded. Many of these social aspects of the environment were established by Mukat.

The Pomo of central California had seven major dialects, seventy-five capital towns, and over five hundred scattered settlements.

In the north, along the Klamath River, tribes speaking very different languages shared a common culture emphasizing a cult of wealth and tradition. More important families generally had their houses positioned higher along the slope of local hillsides.

Leaders held their position through a combination of heredity, generosity, oratorical fluency, and wealth in terms of beads, dentalia, magnesite cylinders, olivella shells, abalone, albino deerskins, and pileated woodpecker scalps. The leader's house was the largest in the community, serving as church and community hall for the larger region.

Many women, particularly after menopause, served as shamans in California. Esoteric priesthoods also occurred. In the south, these belonged to the Chungishnish religion, in the middle to the Kuksu cult, and in the north to World Renewal enactments. Chungishnish involved a grueling initiation in which boys consumed an infusion of datura or jimsonweed to acquire vivid visions. Members re-created a special origin for the world, shared by tribes of southern California, islands of the Pacific, and traditional Japan. This involved the congealing of a primal pair from a total void and the competitive creation of other life forms.

In addition to this origin epic, the story of how Lizard provided the prototype for the human hand is also distinctively Californian.

INTERMONTANE BASIN AND PLATEAU

Framed by the trough of the Rockies, the Basin and Plateau were diverse areas of sagebrush desert. While the Basin has occasional lakes and marshes, water was a vital concern as people depended on a variety of seed and insect crops. Pronghorn antelope and mule deer were the largest species. The Plateau had several species of deer, moose, wapiti (American elk), along with grouse, cougar, and coyote. Salmon from the tributaries of the Columbia and Fraser was the Plateau staple, along with wild root crops like camas and bitterroot.

Couples lived in separate houses, brush shelters in the Basin and long winter mat houses in the Plateau. Men hunted animals and women tended to plants, but during seed or fish harvests, couples worked together. The same happened during net drives for rabbits, antelopes, or birds in the Basin. Men manufactured the tools, built traps, and coordinated their families during an annual cycle of seasonal movements to ripening foods. Women made baskets and blankets, cared for their households, and nourished their kin.

The harvest of each resource was greeted with a First Food ceremony in which that food was taken by the community during a feast to acknowledge their reliance on it. Major trade centers developed in the Plateau at the primary fisheries. At the Dalles of the Columbia, Chinook traders supervised an emporium circulating bison products from the Plains, dentalia from Vancouver Island, slaves from California, and flour made from dried local salmon.

Leaders arose according to the situational needs in the Basin, but came from elite families on the Plateau. All had supernatural sanctions to be successful at a particular task. In the Plateau, the home of the leading family was the largest in the village. There councils and deliberations, involving both men and women, were held. A leader had to be skilled at oratory, generous, senior, and a good example. Often, elite families also included shamans, who worked closely with civil leaders to maintain community standards.

A Plateau Salmon Priest, or Tyee, conducted the First Salmon rite and coordinated activities at weirs and traps during the annual fish runs. In the Basin, specialized shamans conducted communal drives for antelopes. During Winter Dances, Plateau visionaries communally thanked their spirit helpers and renewed the world. In the Basin, any abundance of food was the occasion for a gathering of families to hold a Round Dance or Fandango (a term borrowed from recent Basque sheepherders) to give thanks for their good fortune.

In the southern Basin, Ocean Old Woman is credited with making the world, while in the heart of the Plateau, Sweatlodge is acknowledged. Throughout the area, the actions of Coyote occupy many stories as he made the world ready for humans to occupy center stage. The modern distribution of foods and the techniques for acquiring them were established by Coyote, but so were the possibility of incest, selfishness, and hoarding.

Fine collections of tribal tales have been published by authors well-versed in these traditions. For the Plateau, Mourning Dove, a Colville-Okonogan woman, assembled representative stories from her people, although some that might offend American sensitivities were omitted.

For the Basin, a fascinating collection of commentary and texts from the Chemehuevis, a tribal group from the lower Colorado River area, was presented by Carobeth Laird late in her long life. She had been married to George Laird, a Chemehuevi well-versed in his traditions. Initially, Carobeth was sent by her former husband, John Peabody Harrington, an enigmatic but dedicated linguist and anthropologist, to collect data on this little-known group. By good fortune, Carobeth met George and their collaboration became lifelong.

A skilled writer, Carobeth wrote several books after she reentered California anthropology at the age of seventy-five. Her life with Harrington is described in *Encounter with an Angry God* (1975); a confinement in a nursing home became *Limbo;* and her years with George, who died in 1940, resulted in *The Chemehuevis* (1976), and *Mirror and Pattern: George Laird's World of Chemehuevi Mythology* (1984), based on archival copies of their early work together. She died in 1983, at eighty-seven, while the latter book was in press.

In *The Chemehuevis,* Laird makes clear the pervasive role of oral literatures in defining this and any other Native society. Through males, Chemehuevis inherited certain songs which provided "ownership" of territory and abilities. The two most important of these were the Song of Mountain Sheep or of Deer.

Those who inherited the Mountain Sheep Song (1976: 11) evoked a trail along the west side of the Colorado River in terrain called "my mountain." Those with the Deer Song (1976: 14), went along the east side of the Colorado, following a trail through "my land." Owners of Deer Song also possessed Salt Song (1976: 14), made up of garbled Mohave words. Salt Song was particularly noteworthy because it went through Mohave territory, a region just outside traditional lands, but "claimed" in a spirit of fun. It suggested that the Chemehuevis were true cosmopolitans, playing with foreign words and ranging boldly through enemy territory, to the delight of their sense of humor. The bird song gaiety of the tune made Salt Song particularly appropriate for use on festive occasions (1976: 16).

With equal bravado, this remarkably democratic society included a "high chief," whose few symbols of office included the right to wear turquoise and eat quail beans (black-eyed peas), together with the paramount ownership of a special vocabulary called the Real Song and the Real Speech. As owner of the Talking Song, the high chief was the example upholding the moral code. He had the primary responsibility for setting a high moral tone for his entire community.

For most activities, however, Chemehuevis lived on the land-scape as members of a company (*yunakaimI*), each of which was led by a headman, taking natural resources with the seasons, "repeti-tious, monotonous, yet always surrounded by mystery and spiced with danger" (1984: 123).

Mirror and Pattern is especially good for all the linguistic details so often overlooked in the study of oral literatures, particularly speech signatures. Thus, Coyote prefaces his remarks with haiky*a,* while Skunk inserts haikyaikuku'*u,* Rattlesnake adds a hoarse kwaagwaiw*I,* Chipmunk uses kwivi'*i,* and Duck intersperses kingko'*o* into its words and sentences.

Of special note, Laird also has one of the most sensitive discus-sions of the all-pervasive spiritual aspects of Native life, for humans, shamans (1984: 133, 268), and other life forms. She clearly indicated that the relationship between mythic and present time has only one direction: "The mythic era spills over into the human era, but the reverse is not true" (1984: 17). She adds the insight that "Mythic persons have breath and minds, but they do not have souls" (1984: 18).

During the late 1800s, prophets who arose in the Basin and Plateau had their doctrines carried across Native America. The most famous of these was Wovoka, from Walker River in Nevada, who preached a return to traditions through the Round Dance. His message spread through the Plains, aided by free railroad passes, and, despite the massacre of Lakota at Wounded Knee in 1890, continues to influence beliefs in Western America.

PLAINS

Rolling hills and grassland make up the Plains. In addition to a host of burrowing animals like prairie dogs and gophers, the area was home to millions of bison or buffalo who clustered together and moved north during the summer, but scattered during the winter, moving to the south where they shared the range with antelope.

Initially the home of big game (megafauna) hunters over twelve thousand years ago, Plains river valleys sheltered tribes who lived in earthlodge villages. Each lodge looked like a grassy hill, carefully constructed over a wooden framework and covered with layers of grass, branches, and earth. During the severe winters of the northern Plains, several families stayed dry and warm inside these artificial hillocks. In the south, the warmer climate was matched by more open dwellings, such as the beehive-shaped, grass-thatched houses of the Wichita. Related tribes made houses of wattle and daub or plastered canes. These southern villages were often clustered around earth mounds specially made to raise high their temples, where priests tended sacred fires.

During the summer, these villages were the location of fields of corn, beans, squash, sunflowers, and other crops which grew while villagers left for spring and summer buffalo hunts. The last hunt came in the fall after the harvest.

Men did the hunting and women the farming, although everyone helped out during the seasonal hunts, aiding wherever they were needed. Grandparents often raised their grandchildren because the parents were fully engaged in the arduous tasks required to keep the family fed, clothed, and warm. These farming tribes often traced membership in clans and moieties, commonly called Earth and Sky, through the mother, although some earthlodge tribes emphasized links through the father instead.

With the reintroduction of the horse by the Spanish into the Plains, the same region where the fossil record of its evolution has been discovered, tribal migrations began on a grand scale. Meat became the staple of the diet among these nomadic tribes, while the riverine villages continued to eat a combination of bison and farm crops. Wild berries and nuts also added to the diet, particularly as pemmican, a high energy food made of meat, suet, and berries.

The image of the American Indian as a feather-wearing hunter on horseback, therefore, is only two centuries old. Yet it has become the Hollywood standard. The patterns used, of course, go back centuries, utilizing dogs for the same role later taken by horses. Many Plains tribes still refer to their ancient traditions as belonging to the "dog days" before the arrival of horses. The spread of horses throughout America was often accompanied by the adoption of styles of Plains skin clothing and feathered decoration.

With the horse, temporary dwellings or tents known as tipis could be larger and more stately. During the dog days, they were much smaller. Generally, a married couple and family occupied a tipi. Even the several families who shared an earthlodge would each occupy a tipi while camping on the Plains. While on the communal hunt, families banded together for mutual protection. Among the Lakota, who moved into the Plains from Minnesota, these groups larger than families but smaller than tribes are called *tiyospiye,* and traced descent equally through males and females.

On the Plains, kinship recognized both men and women as ancestors and heirs. The genders were given equal accord in terms of their shared obligations. Complexity derived from the fluidity of the group and the existence of more than just ordinary men and women.

Plains tribes recognized at least six genders, each of which filled a social function. For women, these ranged from that of the virgin who had special roles in ritual, to the wife who kept the household, to the manly-hearted woman who acted more like a warrior male. For men, the range included the contrary who led a life of foolhardy bravery, the husband who kept his family fed, and the berdache who assumed the activities of women and had a vital role in many rituals. Each of these genders was sanctioned by visions and directions from particular spirits. Thunderers, for example, were the patrons of contraries, as was Double Woman for berdaches.

The arrival of new tribes into the Plains increased hostilities. Tribes were often on the defensive and so, in lieu of police or army, men joined a series of military organizations who protected the village, coordinated the hunt, and conducted elaborate ritual displays. These age grade groups were an outgrowth of the mobility and competition among Plains tribes.

During the fall, after the harvest and hunt, villages gathered for their major rituals. In recent times, this has been the Sun Dance, but before the horse, each tribe had its own communal expression, such as the Okeepa of the Mandan, a four-day ceremony enacting the creation of the world and giving thanks to the many species upon which the Mandan relied before they were devastated by a smallpox epidemic in 1837. Only about thirty Mandan survived from a population of several thousand.

Plains tribes spoke of many types of creation. A version from the Hidatsa, close relatives of the Mandan along the upper Missouri River, tells of separate origins for their three villages. The Pawnee had an elaborate creation that began in the sky, and was enacted by means of a complex arrangement of medicine bundles. Living under the full sky of the Plains, star lore played a vital role in orienting people to the landscape and provided guideposts in unfamiliar terrain.

In addition, the Plains was noted for versions of the Flood and for stories rich in the activities of various sets of twins. More recently, accounts of modern-day prophets and a coming ecological disaster have been woven into older traditions of warning and advice told through stories.

SOUTHWEST

The arid climate of the Southwest has become home to a wide variety of cultures. Water is a primary concern, both for people and for crops. Rivers and rain make life possible, but their availability fluctuates. Antelope, rodents, and fish occur in the lower desert, while other animals like deer, cougar, and bear live in the mountains.

A long occupation diverged into several regional patterns. Along the Colorado River, a farming and gathering way of life was followed by the Quechan (Yumans), who benefitted from an annual flooding of the banks that enriched the soil and crops. In the arid south, the O'odam or Pimans gathered and farmed, particularly around an oasis where irrigation would be useful. In the Rio Grande and other rivers, Pueblos developed an elaborate town organization under the control of priesthoods, who worked ritually and socially to even out fluctuations in the climate by supervising irrigation networks and work forces. In the Southwest, men were the farmers. Irrigation and flood control made it labor intensive.

Over six hundred years ago, the ancestors of the Navajo and Apache entered the Southwest and made their livelihood by raiding and farming until the 1680 Pueblo Revolt released Spanish livestock and the Navajo took up sheepherding. Families lived in brush houses, later in round houses called hogans.

Southwestern tribes lived communally. Rich men along the Colorado built large houses where people lived in winter. During the hot summers, a sunshade was all that was needed. O'odam lived in large oval brush houses clustered in villages. The home of the hereditary leader was larger than the others because men gathered there each night to smoke and talk.

Pueblos developed distinctive apartment-style stone and adobe houses. Families lived in a suite of rooms extending from front to back, often with rooms also on lower and upper levels.

Kinship was very complex. Often, Pueblo clans were traced through the mother and grouped into phratries of related or similar kinds. Villages were divided into halves and arranged by membership in kivas, underground circular churches associated with particular tasks or priesthoods. Sometimes clan and household membership came through the mother, while religious affiliation came through the father.

O'odam and Yumans emphasized the paternal line for households, clans, phratries, and moiety halves. Clans owned particular territories and fields which their members were entitled to use.

The clan with the most members usually provided the leader of the community. His home was used for village councils and his family was the custodian of sacred objects associated with local lands and mythic events.

Pueblos have elaborate accounts of how their ancestors emerged from successive lower worlds until they reached the present one. Pueblo creators were often women, who made a world that is then prepared for humans by hero twin boys.

Priesthoods had the responsibility to remember and enact aspects of the life of these twins, while the community itself performed elaborate masked dances reliving features of their ancient history when the Katsina spirits actually lived among them and personally brought rain. Now this has to be done by rituals in which Katsina masks are worn. A thousand years ago, the ceremonial center at Chaco Canyon must have been the location for similar recreations of the world.

The O'odam world was fashioned by Buzzard and Earthmaker

until Coyote and Elder Brother I'itoy made it ready for humans. In the process of killing many monsters, Elder Brother provided petrified hearts and limbs which became the sacred objects of village bundles. The village chief kept these objects in plaited baskets and periodically made offerings to them of black deer tails, eagle down, and beads, praying for the welfare of all his people.

The O'odam world was periodically renewed during the Vikita ceremony for which special songs were composed, ingenious floats were made to be carried around the sacred enclosure, and the sacrifice of children to avert a flood was reenacted in ritual mime.

The Yuman world was made by two brothers who came from the sea, but ritual is concerned with thirty or so Dream Journeys which describe in minute detail the travels of a spirit husband and wife as they visit and name huge stretches of land.

Navajo creation is described in an epic, many of whose incidents also occur in Pueblo and other literatures. Yet the Navajo telling is a bold, innovative, and engaging account that does justice to distinctive features of Navajo life and culture.

Their ritual life is filled with over thirty varieties of chants, each intended to cure a particular dysfunction in a person or a family and to restore harmony to the world.

Among the Apache, however, their major ceremony was held whenever a family invited others to celebrate the coming of age of one or more of their daughters. The Navajo also had the ceremony and it, too, celebrated the efforts of Changing Woman or another female creator to make the world ready for humans. During the girl's puberty ceremony, she was explicitly equated with this all-powerful woman creator.

EAST

Hardwood forests cover the hills and ridges of the East, while rivers and ponds drain its uneven terrain. Its many wild foods were gathered by an ever-increasing population until the introduction of maize, beans, and squash about a thousand years ago reshuffled the population into the Algic, Iroquoian, and Gulf speaking tribes of the historic period. Women took over the chores of farming, while men continued to hunt, mostly deer, during the fall and winter. In the spring, both men and women gathered along rivers and streams to catch and cure fish for storage. In the Northeast, fish runs provided the focus for these activities, but in the Southeast plant extracts were used to kill or stun fish in sufficient quantities to require such labor parties. Along the coast, huge shellfish piles, called middens, indicate that camps along the beaches had been used for millennia.

In the harsher climate of the Northeast, winters were spent living communally in longhouses. These bark-covered buildings had cubicles along either side of a central hallway. Each house was occupied by related women and their families. These female-linked kin formed a matrilineage, which in turn belonged to a matrilineal clan. Often the totem of the clan was painted over the doorways at each end of the longhouse.

Various aspects of nature served as clan totems. Wolf, Bear, Turtle, Snipe, and Snake were fairly common. Within families, membership in each clan was traced through the mother. Hence, the male responsibilities for child rearing and education fell to the mother's brother, rather than to the father, because the former was a member of the same clan as the children but their own father was not. He belonged to his own mother's clan and was responsible for educating and disciplining his sister's children.

After winter was over, families circulated through a series of long-established camps throughout their territories. During the rest of the year, people lived in wigwams, sometimes in tents, set in hunting and gathering areas. Periodically, they would return to the towns where the longhouses and fields were located in order to tend the crops and to harvest them.

The Southeast was also a region with matrilineal clans and towns, but families lived in square compounds with separate buildings on different sides, each with particular functions like cooking, storage, and sleeping. This more open way of living fit better with a warmer climate.

Clans were the basic unit above the household and each clan had a dual leadership consisting of a chief and a captain. The chief led during times of peace, while the captain took over during times of warfare. When peace was declared, the chief made these arrangements and resumed leadership. While the public leaders of each clan were men, it was women who appointed and deposed them. Every clan had a matron who controlled its affairs and kept private tally of its assets and obligations.

During the winter, when blizzards or storms kept everyone close to home, stories were the primary form of both instruction and entertainment. While everyone was together, the full-length versions of legends could be told without interruption.

Stories explained the workings of the universe and human developments. Throughout much of the area, creation was explained in versions of Earth Diver, while Rabbit or Hare served as the primary figure in stories about how the world got to be as it is now.

Each tribe or nation defined itself in terms of an identifying ritual. Throughout the East, this was often a Green Corn Ceremony held just before harvest when the crop was in the milk stage. Still alive and able to receive thanks, the corn ears were soon to be picked for eating and storage. For tribes like the Huron, who lived above the northern limit for farming, the national ritual consisted of the communal reburial of members who had died over a ten-year period. From separate graves, these bones and bodies came to share a common one that became the focus of inter-community sentiment.

Among the Iroquois, a Midwinter rite served as an all-purpose Thanksgiving service for the cosmos. For Iroquois, one of the best known of eastern nations, three epics defined their chronology. First, the earth came to be on the back of a turtle when a woman fell from the sky and was rescued by birds. Her twin sons, Sapling and Flint, fought over the making of the present world and established current activities.

Second, Deganawidah enlisted the help of Hiawatah and Jingonsaseh, the Peace Queen, to form a political union of five tribes and create the Iroquois nation of the Mohawk, Oneida, Onondaga, Cayuga, and Seneca.

Third, in about 1800, Handsome Lake, a drunkard, reformed after a visit from angels who brought him the Good Word. With letters of support from Thomas Jefferson and other officials, he reformulated Iroquois religion and society, permitting men to take over the farming and married couples to live in separate houses of their own.

Among nations of the Great Lakes or Midwest, the traditions of the Winnebago are particularly well known, thanks to a lifetime of friendship, research, and writing by Paul Radin. The Winnebago, whose homeland was Wisconsin, distinguish two types of literature. One is *waikAN* [what is sacred, mythic] set in the irretrievable past and noted for having happy endings; the other is *worak* [what is recounted, historic] set in a time subject to memory, and notable for having tragic outcomes.

The sacred epic describes the creation by Earthmaker, but it was known only by initiated members of the Medicine or Mystic Lodge (Radin 1950), an association of shamans among the Winnebago similar to the Mide [Grand Lodge] of the Ojibway. Interestingly, the story of how Rabbit founded the Medicine Lodge is regarded as historical, not sacred, because it relates to humans. The accounts of the origins of the various clans are also regarded in the same way.

Through an amazing set of circumstances, a published version of Winnebago beliefs exists in print. In *The Road of Life and Death* (1945), Jasper Blowsnake, in a ritual text given to Paul Radin, describes the Winnebago mystic lodge, beginning with various creations by Earthmaker. These beliefs are given form in ritual enactments during the initiation of new members, and evoked again during memorials for deceased members, with a promise of ritual rebirth and renewal.

Blowsnake gave his account only with the greatest reluctance after a series of compelling events. In 1908, the Peyote religion, brought to the Winnebago by John Rave, had a core of strong converts, including men who had been members of the Medicine Rite. In their zeal to spread their new religion, other converts convinced three old men to tell Radin the Winnebago creation saga. These men insisted, however, that they had to leave Wisconsin before doing so.

Thus, on the top floor of a small hotel in Sioux City, Iowa, precisely at midnight, the men began the saga and finished it five hours later. By the next afternoon, every Winnebago knew what had happened and many pressed for a public reading of the text. Until then it had been known only to elite members of the lodge. Agreement was quickly reached and the text was read to a stunned audience. Needless to say, the revealers became the focus of considerable anger, but John Rave stood firmly on their side. Radin left for New York at the end of the summer and the following year more converts were made, including Jasper Blowsnake.

As proof of his conversion, Peyote leaders urged Jasper to dictate the full account for which he had been renowned while a member of the lodge. Jasper agreed to recite the Winnebago words of the rite, but he warned that someone would die from the telling. Radin wrote the text in longhand (this was before tape recorders), working six hours a day for two months. When the recitation ended, Radin learned by telegram that his own father was gravely ill. Within a few days, his father was dead. In addition to his personal sense of loss,

Radin was discouraged because he had a Native text of unusual significance, never to be repeated, but he had no translation of it. Jasper blamed himself for the death of Radin's father. He had warned everyone, but still the text had been written.

Later, in Washington, D.C., Radin received a literal translation of the rite from a visiting Winnebago, but that speaker was not a member of the lodge and did not understand the many esoteric and metaphoric usages.

After much effort, Radin was able to return to the Wisconsin Winnebago. Hearing that the scholar was returning, Jasper fled from him because of the tragic consequences of his former recitation. Soon, however, Jasper took ill and found refuge in the home of a friend. There he decided that telling the Medicine Rite to Radin was "his mission in life."

For the first month, Jasper corrected the prior dictation, while the translation itself took six hours a day for another two and a half months. Lodge members were bitter at Jasper for half a year, but the Peyote believers extolled his courage for a dangerous and heroic act.

According to the narrative, after the creation by Earthmaker, other protagonists engaged in various complex cycles which increasingly rendered the world as it is today. These protagonists are called Trickster, Hare, Red Horn, and the Twins. Radin saw these cycles as comprising a temporal series defining the psychological development and definition of an individual. Each actor gained virtues and character over those who went before.

Trickster lived during a primordial, unformed cosmos of vaguely defined beings. Many of his traits were (or foreshadowed) human ones, but his total being was left unspecified. From the beginning, although he was a chief, all of his actions were contrary to modern injunctions. Some of his adventures were prophetic but others were parodies. All contributed to the further differentiation of the world.

Hare or Rabbit, born of a spirit father and human mother, was raised by his grandmother, the Earth. In his cycle, humans make their first appearance and gain advantages as he matured and learned about parts of his body through a series of misadventures. Through his actions, few of them laudatory, various customs and institutions were created, such as the use of tobacco, bear killing ritual, and menstruation observances, along with the special creation of the Medicine Rite.

Red Horn was heroic, living in a well-differentiated world with a range of defined characters, including humans, monsters, and giants. A majestic figure, his sons avenged his death and revived him. They rid the earth of giants, and received war bundles from Thunderbirds, a great benefit for humans, who come into their own during this cycle.

The Twins (Flesh and Stump) acted juvenile, but with the promise of a new beginning. Their contrasting temperaments caused trouble, until they learned a final lesson from Earthmaker that curbed their unbridled enthusiasm. After killing one of the four animals holding up the earth, they were terrorized by a giant turkey in order that they would know fear. The twins became a culmination of the prior characters, achieving a sense of themselves as individuals. By having at least one adventure with Red Horn, they were also clearly linked with the Winnebago mythic past.

By the end of these cycles, the world was articulated into four levels, each underworld led, from bottom to top, by Turtle, Trickster, Earthmaker, and Rabbit. Supporting our present earth are four island anchors ("island quiet makers"), located at the corners.

Many Winnebago were forced to resettle in Nebraska, but about half of them stayed in Wisconsin. They have seen changes in their land and worked these into their stories, but a better example of this process of changes over time has been documented for New England by William Simmons (1986) in *Spirit of New England Tribes. Indian History and Folklore, 1620–1984.* His examples include oral varieties such as the memorate (a remembered incident), legend, myth, and folktale.

In his overview of the region, Simmons recognized sachemdoms as units of political organization in turn grouped into cultural and linguistic collections known as the Massachusetts, Wampanoag, Mashpee, Gay Head, Narragansett, and Mohegan. Discussing the roles of Pilgrims, missionaries, and colonists, Simmons showed the blending of traditions from England, Africa, and elsewhere with those of New England tribes.

Chapters are arranged in terms of worldview (including pantheon, shamanism, rites, divination, sorcery, curing, and portents), first encounters with Europeans, introduction of Christianity, and texts are arranged by date concerning shamans and witches, ghosts and the devil, buried treasure, giants (Maushop and Squant), little people, and special places. The conclusion discusses the role of stories in the modern Northeast and in the history of these tribes.

An appendix includes other texts that did not fit neatly into prior chapters, providing other aspects of this oral tradition.

Covering stories collected over three and a half centuries, Simmons does a remarkable job of engaging the reader and stimulating the mind as only Native American stories can do.

CONCLUSIONS

Despite these regional differences, none of the stories associated with them can truly be considered unique. Rather, it is the combination of elements and motifs which are distinctive. Incidents come and go with each telling. Factors related to the narrator's personal life, the composition of the audience, the type of setting, and the mood of the overall situation influence each and every recitation. The same episodes, such as Bungling Host, can be found in widely scattered areas, probably because clumsy people are everywhere. An assumed antagonism between water and sky is variously played out across the continent in terms of local fauna. Thunderbirds might be related to eagles or condors, depending on the region, and their foes can range from large snakes to whales.

This dynamic creativity has not received the recognition that it deserves. Often, the incidents now blended together might come from the traditions of the whole world. Adam, Eve, the Ark, and burning bushes have found a place in Indian stories from Maine to Alaska. Rather than taint them, these novel motifs enrich and diversify their appeal.

An important literary device adding to the appeal of these and any other story is reversal. Those hearing a story know they have reached the land of the dead because everything there is backward. Seasons, day, and night were reversed between the land of the living and that of the dead. Animals appeared as humans in their own villages, but as animals around people. What people saw as leaves, Salmon saw as fish.

Certain motifs occur across North America. Among the more significant of these were stories about the origin of death, a flood or deluge, a bungling host, a star husband, an Orpheus-like journey to the afterworld to retrieve a soul, and encounters with a rolling head.

Other motifs have a limited distribution; these included a person swallowed by a monster becoming bald, found in the Northwest

Coast and Siberia; a woman stolen by whales, from the Northwest and Plateau; dog husband, told in the Arctic, Subarctic, Northwest, Plateau, and Plains; and the woman who rejected her cousin, heard in the Northwest, Plains, and Southwest.

Everywhere, stories testify to the importance of interpersonal skills and the tensions inherent in marriage, sex, aggression, altruism, and exchange. In general, these stories express traditional concerns about family life; codify beliefs about the world; suggest alternative solutions; educate the young about proper behavior, names, relationships, and etiquette; entertain people at home or in groups; and provide an emotional outlet for both narrators and audience in a manner that engages the issues without confronting the participants.

PART ONE

MAKING THE WORLD

▼▼▼▼▼▼▼▼▼▼▼

The Law of Conservation, which states that matter cannot be created or destroyed, could have also been expressed by a member of many of the Native communities of the Americas. In its most common form, and, hence, leading off this section, is a version of the Earth Diver, where a living creature goes to the bottom of the ocean to bring up dirt. Powerful forces and much wishful thinking then stretch out this speck to make the earth. The Earth Diver story occurs all across northern Europe and the Americas, as well as Asia. It is among the most famous of human creations.

Alternatively, the earth began when a turtle floated from the depths of the sea and agreed to support land. Many Northeastern tribes share this story. The Delawares trace their ancestry to this turtle and a gigantic cedar tree that grew at its center. The Iroquois and related tribes, who trace kinship through female links, tell of a woman who fell from the sky and found refuge on the turtle's back.

A Void of Nothing was rarely the starting point for creation. Only in Southern California, where the story of Mukat is set, was this notion at all important. Interestingly, similar accounts are also told on Pacific Islands and in ancient Japan. The role of the Pacific in the lives of all of these people suggests that a common version was being shared rather than different stories invented from the logical possibilities of the human experience.

Among Inuit or Eskimo peoples, the basic order of the world was set when Sedna was rejected by her father and sank to the bottom of the sea. In the harshness of the Arctic environment, where life was one of constant danger and threatened by cold itself, it is fitting that survival takes on the larger-than-life dimensions assigned to it in the story of Sedna.

Throughout the East, Hare or Rabbit played a crucial role in establishing the patterns of life. He continues in his more comic aspects as Brer Rabbit, a blending of Choctaw, African, and European incidents along the banks of the Mississippi.

The possibility of other worlds becomes a motif for the various stories of trips into the sky. Marriage to a Star by women from the earth is one of its most frequent expressions. It is told among tribes of the Plains and among those of the Pacific Northwest.

While men and women, animals and plants, old and young are mentioned in all of these stories, they are not humans. They are the people who lived at the beginning. They were—at one and the same time—species, spirits, and shapes with human characteristics. Foremost among these was intelligence. These were people with reason and with intent. What they wanted or wished for was done. They were truly at one with the universe because they were still unformed aspects of it.

Everything they did has consequences today. Everything that they made or said continues, even their mistakes and regrets. Such were the precedents for the making of the world.

CRAYFISH
(EARTH DIVER)
▼▼▼▼▼

"We need a place to rest," all of the fish, water birds, shellfish, and amphibians agreed in council. "We will have to make something solid, something to be called land. How shall we do it?"

A wise fish said, "We cannot make something from nothing. We will have to get something solid already in this world. The sky has nothing and neither does the water. There is only one place to look. That is the bottom of the sea. There is something solid already there."

"But who will get it? None of us can go that deep," questioned a bird. "We will have to ask for volunteers. It is too dangerous a task and may prove fatal. No one can be asked to do this. They can only do it if they want to help all of us. Only if they understand the needs of the greater community can they do this. Who will it be?"

There was a silence.

Then Beaver spoke up. "I will try." And he inhaled several breaths before heading to the bottom. He was gone a long time and people began to worry. Eventually, Beaver floated to the top, dead.

His wife moaned greatly, "Oh, my husband, you were very brave, but it was not to be. What am I to do? What will bring you back? There will be no land. We must learn to make do as we have been doing, floating on the water when we can no longer swim."

An old fish came forward and said, "The world is yet new. If we all sing together, we can restore Beaver to life. Place the body in the middle and gather around it. I will set the tune. All of you follow."

> *Awake. Awake.*
> *There is no death.*
> *Return to life.*
> *Awake. Awake.*

Beaver floated with his hands and feet straight out. After the verse had been sung four times, his fingers began to curl, his elbows and knees began to bend, and his breathing resumed quietly. Four more times and his eyes opened and his mouth began to move. After twelve times, he had a strong pulse and a steady gaze. On the sixteenth repeat, Beaver was singing along, fully restored to life.

Now, Muskrat came forward. "I will try. I am less scared to try because I know all of you will restore me if I fail."

He held lots of air in his chest and dove down. He was gone a long time, a very long time. Then he too floated up to the surface, dead. People gathered his body into the center and began to sing. After sixteen verses, Muskrat revived and was grateful.

Next, Otter said, "I will try. I am quick and lean. I can swim far." Filling his lungs with air, he dove and was gone longer than either of the others. He was gone a very long time. People began to have hope, thinking that he might succeed. But, in time, Otter floated to the top, dead. He was gone so long and went so deep that when they tried to revive him, sixteen repeats were not enough, but twenty verses did restore Otter, who was thankful.

Gloom gathered among the people. No one talked. No one smiled. Everyone thought it was hopeless.

From far in the back, Crayfish came forward and said, "I have been to the bottom of the sea before, but I have not tried to carry anything back. How much dirt do you need?"

The elders talked and decided, "We do not need very much. A handful will do. If we have enough to start with, we can make it expand as needed. Do your best."

"I will try," said Crayfish. "If I do not live, the water here where I went down will turn murky. If I succeed, the water will turn yellowish. Then you will know to act accordingly. If I do not live, you will not be able to revive me. I will have been dead too long before I come to the surface. If I do succeed, you must greet me singing so that I can be revived fully after my exhausting labors."

Without taking a breath, Crayfish dove. He was long gone. People almost forgot that he had undertaken the task. Only a few watched the water. Eventually, they saw it discolor and some thought the worst. A few despaired. Yet the discoloration soon turned yellowish.

"Come back, everyone," the loyal watchers shouted. "Crayfish has gone to the bottom and returns with dirt. The sign is in the water. We must begin to sing as soon as he appears. He needs our help for the last of the effort."

When everyone formed a ring around the yellowish spot, Cray-

fish emerged at the surface with his arms floating straight out and
his tail limp. He did not move. He did not call.

An old man went to the body and said, "Crayfish looks dead. We
have been let down. There will be no solid earth."

Many people began to sob. They could not live as they had been
living. They wanted a change.

The old man inspected the pinchers of Crayfish and found them
empty. "See, it was all for nought. There is no dirt anywhere in his
claws. He made the trip for nothing."

Still, many of Crayfish's friends continued to sing. They sang the
verse, four, eight, twelve, sixteen, and twenty times. There were
small signs of life, but nothing that looked very hopeful. Still they
continued to sing. On the thirty-second repeat, Crayfish revived and
said, "You were too quick to admit defeat. Just because the dirt was
not where you expected it, do not think that I failed. Hold out your
hand, old man, and I will give you dirt."

Amazed, the elder swam forward and held out his hand. From
the juncture where his claws met, Crayfish poured out dirt. He
poured dirt out of each claw.

"This is enough," the old man said. "I will hold it in my hands.
We must all gather around to sing. This song will enliven the earth
and make it spread out:

Alive. Alive.
The earth is born.
It grows solid.
Alive. Alive."

Everyone gathered, with Crayfish near the front. They sang the
song many times. After sixteen times, the dirt began to grow and
firm up. It formed a disk floating on the surface of the water.

When it had filled all of the space occupied by the people, the
old man said, "Climb up onto the earth. Stay in the center. Do not
track mud all over. Stay in the center. Sing some more."

Everyone sang and the earth expanded. Wolf was sent to run in
the four directions. The first few times, he came back quickly and
was sent out again. Still everyone sang. After many trips, Wolf never
came back and they knew the earth was big enough.

Everyone met for a last time to select where they would live in
the world. Some stayed in the water, but many others went to live
on the land. As they took up their abodes, they changed the

landscape. What had been flat and smooth was changed with each settlement. Mountains, hills, lakes, streams, rivers, valleys, and canyons came to be. Plants, Trees, Mammals, Birds, and Reptiles set up their homes.

Eventually, humans also joined them and the world has come to be as it is today.[1]

TURTLE (EARTH GRASPER)
▼▼▼▼▼▼

"Help me. I am falling," cried the woman as she slipped through the jagged hole torn through the sky by the uprooting of the tree of light.

Down and down she plummeted, calling for help.

"Someone calls," shouted the leader of a flock of geese flying through the sky. "We must help them. Close up ranks and form a pad. I see in the distance that it is a woman that falls. She came through that hole in the sky."

The woman landed on the soft backs of the geese and cried out, "Thank you. Thank you. I am with child and my husband flew into a rage when I told him. He leads the sky world and fears an heir. He uprooted the tree that gave us light and shoved me down the hole. I want my child to live."

The leader of the geese flew beside her and said, "There is only water below. There is nothing solid to put you on. We fly all of the time, except when we rest on the sky and clouds. They will not support you. I will fly over the water and ask for help from the beings below. Be patient, we will think of something."

Off went the goose, flying low over the water, calling, "My brothers and sisters under the sea, come up. We have an emergency. A pregnant woman wants a place to stay, a home for her child."

Many heads and eyes came to the surface. One of the largest took charge, saying, "There is only one being that can help us. He lives far below. I will go and ask him."

The head disappeared and was gone a long time. Then the water began to roil and bubble over a large area. Slowly, ever so slowly, a mossy dome emerged from the water. It grew larger and bigger until a huge turtle floated on the surface. "I am here and I will stay floating on the water," the turtle said in a booming voice. "The woman may land and make a home here. I will become the earth. Once my back dries out, I will wish for grass and trees so that she may have food and shelter. Other things will come in time, but it is not for me to decide."

The geese floated lower, waiting for a dry patch to form at the center. There they placed the woman. "Thank you, one and all. Now I can begin life again. My child will have a home."

As trees began to sprout around her clearing, she gathered a bunch of saplings and set one end into the moist earth, twisting them to make them firm. When they formed a double row, she walked down the middle. With strips torn from her dress, she tied the tops together to make a curved roof. From the biggest elm trees she took slabs of bark, easy to peel off because the trees were so new. She covered the surface of her longhouse with these slabs, tying them in place with tree roots she pulled from the ground.

"Now all I need is fire," she thought wistfully. "Then my home will be ready for us to live in. We will be safe and warm."

Even as she thought this, from the edge of the clearing, she saw an old woman approaching, holding a smoldering wad of fibers. As she came near, the old woman said, "I will be grandmother to your sons. I bring you fire. I will keep house and tend the twins while you keep us supplied with food."

They agreed. The woman gathered berries and fruits, while the old woman tended the home. In time, the woman learned the truth of the grandmother's words. She did indeed carry two children, who acted very differently in her womb.

As they prepared to be born, the twins communicated with anger because the expulsion from the sky had divided the initial child. All of the anger of the father had entered one of the twins, and all of the goodness of the mother had entered the other.

The twins talked.

"Move over, you crowd me. I need plenty of room. I am an important person. Get out of my way."

"Relax, brother. We will only be crowded together for a short while more. We must put up with each other until birth. Then you can go your way and I will go mine."

"It won't be soon enough for me. In fact, I see light up there.

That is how I will be born. I'll find my own way out, through that membrane."

"No, no. Not that way, brother. We are meant to be born out this tunnel. We need to leave head first and squeeze out. That is what we must do."

"That's what you think. I am leaving now and I am going out my own way."

The woman writhed on the ground, knowing that she was entering labor. The pain was intense. The old woman came to assist her, but things did not look well.

A bulge developed under the mother's left arm, while a head appeared between her legs. At the same moment, two boys were born, one naturally and one through her left armpit. The mother died.

The grandmother took the twins and washed them in water. She mourned the death and prepared the body. As she sat keening, with the babies beside her, the world seemed a very lonely place.

There had never been a death before. The grandmother was unsure what to do. She wrapped the body in bark and set it aside in the forest.

The boys grew very quickly. Their growth was miraculous. After a day they were toddlers. By the end of a week, they were young men, running and playing.

The grandmother came to favor the one who was left-handed, slighting the one who was right-handed. Lefty was mean and selfish, but the old woman liked him for his arrogance. Righty was kind and considerate, but the grandmother said he was too meek.

The twins vied for her attention. They strove to outdo each other at feats of strength and daring. After about a month, they were men, ready to take on the world.

"Brother," said Righty, "the world is a lonely place. I will make things and beings to fill it and to keep us company."

"What do you say? I alone am sufficient to fill the world. I alone am all that is needed."

"That is not true," replied Righty. "There can be many beautiful and amazing things in the world. We are not enough. The Turtle can hold much more. I will show you."

And Righty sat down after surrounding himself with colored dirt, bark, leaves, wood, and twigs. From these he would make beings, breathing life and thought into them when finished.

Lefty sat across from him with his own pile of makings. "I can do better than anyone. This will be easy."

Righty thought for a moment and began to combine pieces. Soon he had made a long body with thin legs and wide wings. As it came alive, he said, "You will be a butterfly. You will not live long, but you will bring beauty to the world."

Pleased with this model, he made others like it in different colors and shapes. "You will be moths and other pretty wings," he decreed.

Lefty tried to do the same, only his were all legs and head. When he set them free, they buzzed, and swarmed, and bit. They were mosquitos, stinging bees, and bugs.

Righty liked wings and made other creatures. These had feathers and he called them birds. "I will make many different kinds in many colors. You will eat bugs and berries," he said.

Then he moved on to animals. Using sticks and branches, he made legs and tails. From shredded bark, he made fur. He stood them up and pronounced, "You will be deer, and elk, and moose, and beaver. You will eat grass and trees."

Lefty worked furiously on his own. He gave his creations legs and tails, along with fangs and claws. "See," he said, "I can do better than you. I have made fierce animals who will eat yours. They will be bobcat, cougar, bear, and badger."

The animals scattered to their new homes all over the world. They kept far apart for some time. Eventually, some died or were killed. Others took their places.

The twins continued their contest.

Righty took green earth and straight fibers and made corn. Then he made vines with squash and pumpkins, plants with beans, and tobacco. These he told, "Take root wherever you can. Grow big. You will be siblings, feeding everyone to come."

Lefty saw the vines and thought to do the same. He made poison ivy and other plants that cause painful welts and itches. "Grow everywhere and take over," he said. "Through your efforts people will remember me." And thus it has been since.

Lefty knew he had not done well, but Righty did not accuse him of doing harm. He kept his peace. Instead, he made herbs and medicine plants to treat bites, scrapes, broken bones, and irritations.

Lefty brooded on his shortcomings. He was much better than his brother, yet he had not been able to prove it. His grandmother took his side, but with all these new creatures filling the earth, he was outnumbered. His brother now had many friends. They gave him a new name, to honor his support of the good life. They named him Sapling.

Their father's anger had created Lefty and the successes of the good twin had unleashed it. As he brooded, Lefty became more and more incensed. He plotted revenge. When he asked their grandmother for help, she refused, saying, "I am scared of this new world. If I do wrong, I will be punished. If I help you, I might die. Do whatever you want by yourself."

Extremely angry, Lefty went off into the woods. There he found Sapling praying at the grave of their mother.

"Now I will show them," he threatened. "I will show them both. Praying is not the way to treat the dead. I will show you how to treat them," he screamed as he rushed toward the body.

He threw off the wrappings and grabbed the head. He pulled it off. He kicked it. He kicked it around the clearing. He kicked it into a tree and it lodged into the upper branches.

Sapling was stunned. Grandmother wailed. She cried and she mourned. She sang a weeping song. As she sang, the skull rose into the air. Higher and higher it went, up into the sky. It became the Moon.

Sapling wrapped up the body very carefully. He decreed, "This must not happen again. Henceforth, the dead will be buried. Bodies will rot and skeletons will turn to dust. Only enemies will have the anger to mutilate the dead. The corpse must be respected. It must return to the earth and share in the creation of new life. That will be how things will be done."

Then Sapling turned on his brother. "I have accepted many mean and hurtful things from you. I have put up with your arrogance and your selfishness. I have tried to accommodate you. I have tried to think well of you. From now on I cannot. You have done too much. You have spoiled the earth. You have insulted our mother. This is the end. Now we will fight."

Lefty fled in fear. He became a coward. He went deep into the woods and he plotted revenge, sneaky and cowardly revenge. He decided to gather up all of the birds and animals and to hide them in a cave under the earth. He invented soft music to do this. He lured all of the creatures into the cave and he sealed it up.

Sapling and grandmother began to starve. The world began to wilt. Even the water began to dry up. No birds sang. No herds grazed. No insects buzzed. All was quiet, still, and uncertain.

Sapling went hunting for his brother. He invented weapons. Spears, bows, arrows, knives, and clubs he took along. He went far to the east, but could not see him.

With only the light of the Moon, things were murky. At the

eastern edge of the Turtle, Sapling made the Sun. He took shells
and foam and gleam. He made a ball and he enlivened it. He sent
it into the sky, saying, "You will travel from east to west each day.
You will bring bright light. In the evening, you will set in the west.
At dawn, you will rise in the east. You will be the Sun. What you
do in the day, the Moon will do in the night."

He went back home. The next morning, at daylight, he went to
the south. He looked all day, but he did not see his brother. He
went home by moonlight.

The third day, he went west. Again, he found nothing. He went
home.

The fourth day, he went north. He looked very carefully because
the cold winds of that direction were made by his brother, along
with severe winters. Surely, Lefty would hide in the north. Far into
the cold Sapling went, but he could find nothing. Lefty had covered
his tracks well.

Sapling had stretched the world as he had walked in the four
directions. Now it was big enough to allow animals to reproduce
on their own. To live and die by natural means.

He paused to consider his quest for his twin and the animals and
decided that he had gone about it wrong. He had looked through
the world guided by light. Now he would look for darkness.

He sought out the dark. He looked for the darkest places and,
very shortly, he found his brother, guarding the sealed entrance to
the cavern. Inside he could hear the muffled sounds of herds of
animals milling around in the dark.

"Brother," Sapling cried, "I have come to fight you to the death.
I have come to free life from your trap. I have come to set the world
right. I cannot undo your errors, but I can put an end to you and
any further plans. I challenge you."

"But I now own all the animals," his brother mocked. "They are
mine. I have no need to fight. I have what I want and I can wait for
everything else to wilt and die. Then I will be undisputed master of
the world. Grandmother will come back to me and I will have all
that I need."

"That is why I fight you now. Nothing further will wilt. Things
will reverse. They will grow and prosper. This will become a good
place for humans to live. I raise my club and I will strike the first
blow if you do not rise and defend yourself."

"I am unarmed," his brother mocked. "How could you hit
someone who is defenseless?"

"Because it needs to be done," replied the good man. And he

raised his club and moved to strike. In that instant, the brother willed to himself, "I will now be coated by a hard shell." And he was. This coating deflected the blow and left him unhurt.

"My skin is hard and my hands are knives," he shouted. Then he lunged for his brother and cut him.

The battle raged for hours. Hunks of the bad twin were knocked off and scattered over the ground. These became the first rocks. Sapling relied on the healing herbs that grew around them to treat his own wounds and staunch the flow of blood. The other brother had no such recourse. Poison ivy and mosquitos gave him no solace. Eventually, he was defeated.

Sapling released the animals. As they came through the entrance, each one split in two, forming a male and a female. These became the parents of each species.

Finally, Sapling turned to his brother, crumpled on the ground, and said, "From now on you will do some good, although you will still occasionally hurt. You will be Flint. People will use you for sharp edges and chipped tools. Sometimes you will wound, but mostly you will help."

And so the world was made ready for humans.[2]

MUKAT
▼▼▼▼▼▼

Silence. Darkness. Nothing. Not a sound. Not a motion. For eons there was nothing.

Ever so gradually, there was a flicker, a tiny shiver of motion. It became a quiver, a swirl. Something congealed. It fell and was egg-like. Nothing happened to it. It was a miscarriage.

Nothing.

Then it happened again. Very slowly, a twitch became a shake. A flutter became a swirl. Something dropped, egg-like, to hover in the air.

Inside were two beings, lying together. They grew and grew until they became big. Their size broke the egg.

MUKAT 51

"I am the older," one said. "No, I am older," replied the other.
Then they heard a noise. "Listen," they said to each other.

Night was singing. The pair floated quietly, listening.

Finally, one said, "What shall we do?"

"We should make the earth," said the other.

Singing, each of them produced a cane. Making the canes stand
steady, they built the earth on top of them. One made the lighter
part; the other made the darker part.

Then water flowed from the noses of these beings, who told it
to run over the earth in patterns. All was ready.

"Now, we will make people," they agreed. Clay was molded into
shapes. Then they stopped to smoke. From the smoke, they made
light, including the Sun, a man, and the Moon, a woman.

They looked at the shapes. One had made people whose bodies
each had many arms, legs, eyes, and ears. The other had made them
with two of each. He was Mukat, and he determined the correct
shape of these creations. Yet disagreements continued.

"There should never be change or sickness. There will be no
death," demanded the other.

"That is not good," said Mukat. "There needs to be change and
sickness. People need to learn to care for each other. Some will die.
That will make room for children. Younger generations will take
the place of older ones."

Angry, the other of the pair took his creations and went into the
ground. He left. He tried to take the entire sky with him, but Mukat
held it back. He struggled to keep the sky, and he did.

During the struggle, there was an earthquake. Rocks piled up.
Fissures cracked the earth. Terrain was roughed up and made
uneven.

Then it was quiet. Four of the creations of the other one were
left behind. These were Coyote, Palm, Eagle-Flower, and Fly. These
had clung to Mukat during the trembling.

The Sun fled during the terrible shaking, but the Moon stayed
in the sky. She looked at all the people when it was quiet and she
decided to cheer them up. "Everyone, gather around," she called. "I
will paint each of you in many interesting colors and patterns."
Everyone had a good time.

Mukat became concerned that people would want to stay just
this way forever. He invented bows and arrows. He had everyone
make them. Then he said, "Divide in half. Make two teams. Form
sides and shoot one another. It will be fun." They did this and

thereby formed the two sides, Coyotes and Wildcats, that continue to organize their lives.

People shot at each other, but the dead did not revive. Many people died forever. These became noisy ghosts who roamed the earth. They bothered the living. Soon, people learned to ignore them and the ghosts went to live under the ground.

People had a meeting and decided, "We must kill Mukat. He cannot be trusted. Who will do the deed?" No one answered.

Finally, Woodpecker urged, "We need to use sorcery. That will kill him."

Lizard volunteered, "I will watch Mukat and find a way to get at him."

Night came. Moon had everyone gather to dance and sing. Mukat kept to himself. He slept by himself in the desert. Late at night, he got up and using his cane, he hobbled to the ocean where he defecated.

Lizard told everyone, "We can get what Mukat eliminates from the ocean. We can use it to do him in. That part of him can be used for evil. Now we must decide who will get the foul stuff."

After due consideration, Frog was asked to hide in the ocean and steal some of Mukat's feces. He agreed.

Late the next night, Mukat went to the ocean, but Frog was waiting for him, hiding on the bottom. As Mukat hobbled with his cane, he became unsure of his footing. Frog did not feel like the sandy bottom. Mukat's cane poked Frog many times, leaving the spots that frogs have today.

Still, Frog waited until Mukat was done. Angry, Frog grabbed more feces than he intended. He took it to noxious creatures and they mixed up a potion. They willed Mukat to die.

Mukat became very ill. He could not move. Coyote pretended to befriend Mukat and take care of him. Instead, Coyote stole more of Mukat's leavings and made him much worse.

As he neared death, Mukat called everyone together. "I will soon die. I know that Coyote wants to eat my body, but he must not. He will abuse what power comes to him. Keep him away. Find my creations called Fire and Rock. Use them to burn my body. Save my power." Everyone agreed.

Mukat died. Coyote sat among the mourners, waiting his chance, but they sent him on an errand far away. After he had traveled some distance, Coyote looked back and saw smoke rising from the pyre. He ran back as fast as he could. Most of Mukat's body was consumed, only a bit of heart was left. People formed a ring around the fire, trying to protect the body.

Coyote was too fast. He jumped over the ring of people and he stole the heart. Everyone chased him, but he got away. People began to weep continuously in sorrow.

Coyote took clay and invented pottery so he could store the heart. When it was safe, Coyote removed the heart and ate it.

Then Coyote traveled on. As he went, he became more tired. He became ill. He got thin. He became delirious. He made outrageous demands on people. He did senseless things.

Finally, he went to the ocean and gathered many pretty and valuable objects. He made a wooden figure of Mukat. He dressed and painted it.

Coyote came home and announced, "Everyone, gather around. We will hold a memorial feast. We will visit with our creator one more time. Then we will burn up all of these jewels as offerings." They held the first Mourning ceremony. This made everyone feel better. They stopped weeping. Then Coyote went away.

Now the world was ready for the ultimate change. People decided to turn into other creatures. They became animals, plants, rocks, trees, stars, and weather. They are that way still.[3]

SEDNA
▼▼▼▼▼▼

"Come, Daughter," the man said, "there is an animal on the beach that I killed and it needs to be cut up and stored."

"Thank you, Father," she replied. "It will be good to have fresh meat to cook. The storm of the past few days has depleted our supplies. We also need oil for our lamp. Rendering blubber will provide it."

"You are wise to plan ahead, Sedna," her father responded as he went to rest from his grueling hunt. "You have been a wonderful daughter since your mother died. I, too, thank you in return."

At the beach, Sedna began to cut up the body with her ulu (crescent knife) and prepared to give hunks of meat to various people in the camp. That is what Inuit (Eskimo) did whenever there was fresh meat.

Many men came to court her, but she never found one to her liking. Her father was also reluctant to give her up, so the decision was hers alone as to whom and when she would marry.

After she had cut up and distributed most of the meat, a handsome man came up to her and watched. He was a seabird.

Softly, he said, "Come with me to our village across the water. There is lots of food. We never lack for meat or oil. Our beds are covered with thick bearskins. Our clothes are the softest feathers. You would never want or lack."

He was very strong and handsome. He was a great hunter. She was convinced. She went back to her tent and said, "Father, I have decided to marry. I am going across the sea to live with the seabirds. They promise me plenty. Your sister will care for your needs until you can marry again."

Reluctantly, her father agreed. He knew this day would come and he hoped for grandsons to feed him in his old age. He wished her well and urged, "Sedna, I want you to be happy. Take your clothes, a lamp, and a stone pot. Everything else will be supplied by your new husband. That is our way."

She went with her husband. After many days of hard travel, they crossed the frozen sea. She was exhausted.

"Here is our home," the man said. "It is now yours to take care of. You are wife here."

Amazed, she looked around. Then she dropped to her knees and sobbed. In time, she moaned, "I have been deceived. This tent is made of mangy fishskins. They are full of holes and the wind blows through. The skins on the bed are worn and thin. The clothes are made of moss. There is no food. What am I to do?"

"This is how we live," her husband replied. "You are now my wife and this is how you will live, too. We have lots of food. We eat minnows. You will get used to it here."

"My pride has gotten the better of me," Sedna cried. "If my father knew, he would rescue me. I am alone now. I did this to myself. I will resist for as long as I can, but eventually I will have to live as you do. I know that. I do not like it, but I know the truth. Give me a few days to adjust. Leave me alone. Then we can live together."

"Indeed I will," the seabird answered. "I want you to be content, but you have very few choices. There is nowhere to go. Make yourself at home."

Sedna pouted for a few days, but soon she was too busy to dwell on her fate. She made fish glue and patched the tent. She got tiny plants from the tundra and stuffed the beds. She learned to eat minnows.

After a year, Sedna longed for her father and wished for him to visit. During warm weather, the sea cleared and the father set out in his boat to travel. The way was long, but not as dangerous as crossing the ice.

As he landed on the beach, Sedna rushed to him, sobbing, "Father, I did wrong. I was prideful and willful. This is not a nice place. I have done my best, but our house is flimsy, our clothes are disgusting, and the food is bad. My husband tricked me. I do not want to stay. Take me home. I will care for you as before. I will do better than before."

The old man looked around and saw that she told the truth. Without a word, he helped her into the boat and shoved off. They paddled away.

"If I had stayed," he said to her, "I would have killed your husband. I would have avenged your treatment. I would have committed a crime. All that is important is that you are safe. When we get home, we can talk more about this."

Later, when the seabirds got home, they noted the drag marks on the beach and knew that Sedna had left. "She will insult us," they all agreed. "She will mock us. She will spread lies. We must prevent that." They flew over the ocean until they found the boat, then they summoned up a tempest.

"We will die," cried Sedna.

"Only if I do not return you to the birds," shouted her father as the waves towered over the boat. He grabbed Sedna and tried to throw her overboard. Instead, she clung to the side of the boat with her hands.

"You must go back," her father cried. "You made your choice last year. Now the birds have used their powers to remind you of your commitment. You have a husband and relatives with the seabirds. You must go back to them or we will all suffer."

Sedna held on all the tighter. Her father could not wedge her loose. In desperation, he drew his knife and began to cut off her fingers, one at a time.

The first finger of one hand became seals. All of the other fingers of that hand became other sea mammals.

The first finger of the other hand became caribou, and the rest became other land mammals.

Without fingers, Sedna could not hold on and she sank into the sea. As she went down, the seabirds ended the storm. They had accomplished their purpose.

"I will not die," Sedna prayed as she sunk to the bottom of the ocean. "I will live here and I will control all the animals. People who are good husbands and wives will be able to eat meat. I will see to that. Bad people will not eat my food. They will perish. People must keep my gifts apart. Seafood must never be cooked in the same pot with land food. That is taboo. If people do that, my hair will tangle. Since I cannot comb it, I will get angry. I will withhold the game. I will punish the people. Only if a shaman comes to me and asks for meat while combing out my hair will I relent. That is now the law of the world."[4]

HARE
▼▼▼▼▼▼

"Mother, please take me with you," asked the girl. "You always go off all day long to dig wild potato roots. When you come back, I help you lay them in the sun to cook, but I can also help you dig. We can get more roots that way."

"No, Daughter," answered the mother. "That is what I do. I dig the potatoes with my digging stick. Your job is to stay home and wait until I return."

"But I am bigger now than I have ever been. I can be a real help. I can lighten your load. I am young and strong, and you are not. Please let me go. Please let me help."

"Very well, but I will send you home if you look tired," said the mother.

They went some ways around a hill and along a stream until they came to a damp ravine.

"Here is where I always come," cautioned the mother. "There are ample potatoes here, but you must observe certain rules. You must face only south. I am nervous that you will ignore this rule, so I was reluctant to have you come along. You must always remember to face south. Prove to me that you can be trusted."

"You can trust me. I am old enough to understand," the girl assured her parent.

"So be it," said the mother. "You dig here, and I will go down a ways and dig there. Observe my warning."

The girl dug with dedication, mumbling to herself, "Such exercise is good for me. It is much better than waiting at home. These potatoes are nice and big. They virtually pop out of the ground when I probe with my digging stick. My mother was very kind to bring me and I will repay her with lots of food."

Delighting in her freedom and the value of her efforts, the girl let her mind wander. In time, she let the locations of the roots determine her movements. Soon she was facing north.

Whoosh. Whoosh. Whoosh. Whoosh. A great rushing, roaring, and howling came from the north. The wind became a cyclone and picked up the girl, who screamed, "Mother! Mother! Help! Help!"

Her mother rushed to her.

"Hold me by the shoulders. Keep me down. Hold me as tightly as you can."

Her mother grabbed the daughter with one hand and a tree with the other, screaming back, "Now you see why I did not want you to come? You should have stayed home. You are being punished for your disobedience."

Then it suddenly became still and very, very quiet. Mother and daughter stood stock still. After a few moments in rigid positions, the mother said, "Gather up all the potatoes we dug. Let us hurry home." And they did.

The next day the woman went out alone, and the daughter stayed home, as it had always been. They went back to the old pattern.

Several months later, early in the morning, the girl woke her mother up. "Mother, I feel very strange. I am not myself. Something is moving inside of me." Then her mother knew that the girl was pregnant and prepared accordingly.

The girl was kept in her warm bed and the fire was built up. The mother prayed and sang. In a vision, she learned that the four winds had fathered the children to be born.

Soon the girl went into labor. The firstborn was a powerful being who could take the form of a small white Hare with trembling ears. The second was a similar being who could assume the shape of a Wolf. The third was a flint knife, which killed the woman who had given it birth. Since then, birth has been dangerous, sharp-edged, and painful.

Hare grew quickly and set about making the world. When he had difficulties because of his enthusiastic stupidity, Wolf came to his rescue.[5]

STAR
▼▼▼▼▼▼

"It has been a hard day and I am very sleepy," one sister said to the other. They were camping away from home, up in the hills, so they could gather berries for the winter.

"It is a warm night," the elder sister said. "Let's sleep outside under the sky. I'll move our mats out of the tent and you bring the robes because it might get cold before morning."

"Good idea," agreed the younger one. "If we sleep over there in the hollow, we will also be protected if the breeze turns into a wind."

Soon their beds were made and they were nodding off. Just as the older was falling asleep, she yawned and said, "Look up, sister. See those two big stars. One is bright red and the other is dull white. Don't you wish that we were married to them? Then we would have help with the heavy work, lots of meat, and warm beds."

"Oh, you silly woman," mumbled the younger sister, "if we were married to those stars we would have even more work to do. We would have to keep house better than we do. We would have husbands to feed, and we would have children to care for all of the time. Remember what our mother always said. Be careful what you wish for, otherwise you might get it and rue the day of your presumption. Take care and don't be silly. Go to sleep. Now."

But the Stars had heard and they, too, wanted wives. So, while the sisters slept, they floated up into the sky and each came to rest in the bed of one of these two men.

With the dawn, the sisters awoke.

"My wish came true," exclaimed the older woman. "Here is a fine handsome man to be my husband." Then she looked across the way and saw the man married to her sister and moaned, "Oh, no."

The other sister was awakened by the familiar voice and rolled over to look at her husband. She began to cry. "Woe. Misery. Here is a very old man with drippy eyes. It looks like pus."

Angry, she looked at her sister and cried, "This is all your fault. You wished for this and now see what happened to me."

"No, this is all your fault, younger sister. You did not wish for the best. You got what you deserve."

At the sound of angry words, both men awoke. The young man said, "We are both fine husbands. Give us a chance. The old man may not look handsome, but he has many skills and talents and will keep all of us well fed. Trust him."

"Oh, but he is ugly," cried his wife. "I want a handsome husband like you. Can we exchange or can you marry me, too?"

"No, that cannot be," explained the young man. "In the sky there are so many stars that we can only have one spouse each. Otherwise there would not be enough husbands or wives to go around. The old man has already been married, and happily, too, but his wife became a shooting star and so has left us. I was waiting for a wife and now one has come. Dry your eyes and make the best of things. It will not be as bad as you think."

"Yes, do that sister," coaxed his wife. "We will now live in the sky and do what we must as married people."

Still, the younger sister cried and they left her alone. The men took the older woman on a tour of her new homeland. By the time they returned, the other sister was resolved to make the best of things.

"Good, my wife," said the old man. "I am not mean or hurtful. I will be a good husband. I only ask that you help out here with the food and house. I will do the rest. Here in the sky, women dig roots for our food and grind them up to make biscuits. I only ask that you not dig roots that go straight down or that grow deeply into the soil. Those are not very tasty and should be avoided."

"I am used to helping out. I will do as you say," his wife responded. "I only ask that you sleep apart from me. I do not want to get that close to you and your dripping eyes."

"I will do as you ask. It will not hurt me," the old man said. "We have already spent a night together and you will have my child. I am pleased."

Again the younger woman began to sob. "I am not ready to be

a mother. I do not want a child. How can this be? Take it away."

"No. That cannot be," the young man challenged. "Children are needed in any world. It will be healthy and strong. You will bear it and we will raise it. We are a family."

Turning to the older sister, his wife, the man said, "I think your sister is spoiled and irresponsible. Shall we send her back?"

"No. Please do not do that," pleaded the older sister. "She was raised by a loving family and was always the youngest. She was indulged, but she was not spoiled. She knows that her place is to help and to share, and she will do so. Won't you, sister?"

Taken aback by this discussion in front of her, the woman could only nod in agreement. "I am ashamed," she muttered, but, even so, she plotted in her head to escape.

"Come, sister," said the elder one. "Let us dig roots for our supper." And the sisters went off.

When they were far away on the plain, the younger sister spoke earnestly to her sibling. "I truly do not like it here. Why can't I go home? Why can't you help me?"

"It is not a good idea," the other explained. "I will be lonely without you and it would not be safe for the baby. Please consider your responsibilities here. We are married now and have to act mature."

"I will try, but I do not think it will work. I am unhappy and homesick. Life below was better than this."

Still, the sisters took up the task of digging roots for their meal. The bulbs were large and fresh, much better than those on earth. The sisters wandered apart as they dug more and more roots. When both baskets were filled, they went home.

Their husbands had been out hunting and they also returned with food for the meal. The sisters butchered the game and hung some meat slabs up to dry. A few steaks they put on to cook, along with a kettle of roots and spices. They did not grind the roots and make biscuits that night.

Supper was quiet, with little discussion. Afterward, the men smoked while the women cleaned up the dishes. Then, when it became dark, the couples went to bed, only the old man and his wife slept separately.

At first light, the women were up, feeding the fire and getting ready for the day. They went to the stream to bathe. Then the men got up and bathed separately. After only a cold snack, everyone went out to get food. They did this for a week.

One morning, the younger sister said, "You realize, sister, that we now have to travel further and further from our camp in order to get enough roots. Soon we will have to move camp to a new location. How do we know what other people are here? We see only our husbands. Are there enemies? Friends? Monsters? Who can say? Surely you must realize that our husbands are hiding something. Don't you want to leave? I still do."

"Stay calm," said the older one. "You make too much of things. We are living and eating well. Things are pleasant. Why can't you be content?"

"This is not our home," the younger sister stated.

"It is now," replied the elder.

The sisters continued to dig and talk because the plants were close together in that section.

Suddenly, the younger dropped to her knees and said, "Oh look, here is a root that grows straight down. I am following it, the soil is very loose and keeps slipping away. Where does it go, I wonder?"

"Don't do that. We were forbidden to dig roots like that. They are not good to eat. We were warned. Stop!" shouted the older sister.

"You are too late. Now I know why we were warned," gasped the younger. "The root made a hole in the sky and I can see the earth. I am looking down at our village. I cannot make out the people, but I can see tiny ant-like figures walking on two legs. I can study the village and I know where our house is. I can almost see our family. Oh, sister, I truly want to go home. There are lots of people there and I will not feel so lonely."

"Move over," said the older. "I want to see. Indeed, that is our home. That is where we came from. It looks so nice and pretty. I can see our house, our home. You are right. That is where we belong. Maybe our husbands will come back with us. We could go there as married people."

"But that cannot be," explained the younger sister. "Those men are stars. If they come to earth, they will die. Remember that the wife before me became a shooting star and was lost to them. Only we can go back, with my child. He or she will only half belong to the sky. We cannot tell our husbands. We must work in secret. Be careful. I will cover up this hole so that no one will know we know about this possibility. Meanwhile we will plan our escape."

"What can we do?" pleaded the older.

"I have a plan. If you will dig more roots every day to fill both baskets, I will braid fine tree roots into a cord that will reach to the ground below. It will take time, but we will be able to climb down then."

After digging for a few more hours, the sisters went back to their camp to prepare supper. Over the meal, the old man said suspiciously, "You women must know that it is very still here. We are above the clouds so our weather is always the same. Yet this afternoon, there was a breeze. That is very unusual here. Do you know anything about it? Have you been careless with nature?"

"But we felt no breeze," replied the sisters. "We were out on the plain for hours and the weather was always the same. We noticed no change."

"Well," hinted the man, "be careful. Things in the sky have a certain way about them. They cannot be upset."

"But we do not really know the way of the sky," defended the older sister. "You say there are many stars, but all we have seen are you two. Where are the others? Are they friend or foe?"

"Oh," said the old man. "You must understand that with so many stars we like to live far apart. If we lived close together, our light would not be clear and precise. We would look hazy or like a blob. We would not make up many fine dots in the sky. We neither like nor dislike each other. Sometimes we visit, but we do not stay long. When the child is born, he will live with us, but when he is grown, he will have to go far away to have a place of his own."

"But that is cruel," cried the younger sister. "On earth, our children stay with us and take care of us as we grow older. That is what makes us a family."

"But that is not the way of the sky. That is why our son will leave eventually."

Disheartened, the younger woman was mute, as was her sister. After cleaning up, everyone went to bed, but the older sister slept away from her husband for the first time.

In the morning, at the digging ground, the older sister said, "Now I know that you were right, sister. Things are too strange here for us to stay. We will follow your plan. I will dig extra roots to fill both baskets, and you will make cord to get us home."

And for weeks that is what they did. As more and more rope was made, they had to disguise it as a hill, covering the surface of the heap with loose soil and a few well-placed plants.

"My stomach continues to grow," said the younger. "It is well that I get to sit here making rope, otherwise I would soon become exhausted from the labor of bending over and reaching down. I can barely see my feet."

"I wish it were the same for me," moaned the older one. "I get lots of exercise, but doing double the work means I am twice as exhausted at night. Still, it is for a good cause. Soon we will escape. It will have to be during the day. Probably at noon because then the stars are away or hidden and we will not be seen."

"I agree," echoed the pregnant one. "I only ask that I go first because I so want to go home."

"You will get your wish soon enough," said the elder. "Just keep braiding and twisting, while I keep digging."

Finally, their hill had gotten quite high and they thought there was enough rope to reach the earth. On the day they set to leave, they did everything as usual in the morning. They fed the fire, bathed, and fed a cold snack to the men. They wandered out onto the plain, and began to move as though digging roots. They kept near the hill until noon.

"Now," whispered the younger, and the older sister agreed.

They rushed to the hill and brushed off the dirt. One end of the rope was tied around a huge tree and the other was taken to the place nearby where the covered hole was.

"Quickly, uncover the hole," the younger urged. "Place the end of the rope into it and shove the rest down as fast as you can. When most of it is through, I will grasp the rest and start down." And that is what she did.

Meanwhile, the old man tensed in the forest where he was. He called to the younger husband, "Come quickly. The breeze is back and I fear the worst. The women are trying to escape and will kill themselves. We must save them and drag them back. We need my son if our own plans are to be successful."

Together the men rushed into the breeze and soon came to the hole, only to find a rope sticking out and tied to a tree.

"Now they have done it," screeched the old man. "Let me see how far they got. They cannot have reached the lower earth, yet."

The younger man leaned over the hole, while the old man looked down. Far below they saw the older sister. And far below her was the younger one.

"Let us teach them a lesson," snarled the younger husband as he reached for the rope. They had no knives and could not untie it, so they began to shake it. As the tugs began to move down the rope, it began to sway back and forth more and more rapidly.

"They are after us," cried the older sister. "They want to throw us off. They want to kill us. Hang on. Hang on tightly for dear life."

"I hear you, sister, but I am almost there. It is you who must be careful. Don't look down and be sure to hang on. I can see some of our relatives rushing to the end of the rope. They cannot reach it. It is not long enough. Our father is coming with a hide and he will have everyone hold it so that we can jump and be saved. Just come down closer, sister."

As she spoke, the wave action of the rope reached her. She was ready and hung on tightly. Soon her feet were at the end of the rope and she looked down.

"Jump, daughter, jump," shouted her father. We have a skin stretched tightly and it will break your fall." And it did.

In a short time, the older sister did the same.

From the ground, everyone looked up into the sky to see two tiny faces scowling at them. Then they disappeared.

Ever cautious, the father warned everyone, "Go back home. Quickly. Those men have gone to get knives and they will cut the rope. When it falls it will kill whatever it falls on. Go home and hide."

Everyone did just that. When the rope fell, it made a tremendous noise and created a mountain where none had been. The dirt that had covered the rope in the sky world turned to stone in this one, but many rats soon came to live there because they discovered that if they burrowed into the mountain there was lots of rope to chew up.

The sisters soon married human husbands, but when the boy was born and grew up, he was always looking at the sky. In time, he became the astronomer of the tribe and he helped advise the chief and predict the winds, tides, and seasons.[6]

PART TWO

ADJUSTING
THE WORLD

▼▼▼▼▼▼▼▼▼▼

Since many aspects of the earth were there from inception, the next
phase of creation had to do with making them more widely available, with sharing what was already there in limited ways, and with
giving everyone free access to necessities.

Selfishness was the great adversary. Couples would hoard, each
dispensing when and what they wanted, but keeping secret their
source. The chief virtue of the heroes of this time was their willing-
ness to free up a place, food, or material, while poking fun at the
pretensions of those who tried to lord it over others. Equality and
democracy were being forced on tyrants. Ways were made straight
and open. Distinctive abilities were lauded, individuals were encouraged, and all worked toward a common good.

Throughout western America, Frog had a close association with
fresh water and with fire. Being amphibious, such contradiction was
second nature. In this story, combined from many sources, Frog
leads a band of heroes to the sky to bring back fire. The selfishness
of Mrs. Bear stands out in contrast to the generosity of the Giants.
This is not always the case. Selfishness was everywhere in those
days. Life could not go on unless things improved. Our world was
a damp and murky place until people cooperated to make it better.
Light and warmth were major improvements.

Always cast as best friend, unless the story is told from the
standpoint of Wolf and Coyote, Dog figures as the hero who foils

the Buzzards and releases all the game in this Caddo story. Far from being a canine turncoat who exchanged his freedom for a warm bed and steady diet, Dog takes the initiative here.

Coyote, who plays the role of hero, trickster, shaper, and transformer throughout the West, humiliates the Swans by thwarting their elite pretensions, but, in typical Coyote fashion, he does so on his own terms. Another version of this story was told among the Salishan tribe at Arrow Lakes. Many volumes have been printed to chronicle the deeds and misdeeds of Coyote. His figure was a pivot for all kinds of changes and absurdities.

Many tribes have named heroes who make their world a better place. The Kootenay of the Canadian border area between Montana and British Columbia have a complementary pair. Names were established from the beginning. To name something was to give it power and identity. This was basic to the differentiation of life. Shaper took on the responsibility of releasing particular hoards. He made flint, foods, and fashions widely available, but, as with any strong-willed person in a community, his ways were not always those of others. He just had more important connections.

The human body was increasingly the basic form for these beings. The shape was mobile but defenseless. Frail and lacking claws, horns, or fangs, the human body was the essential form for all other beings. Among the few improvements that appear in stories is the gift of Lizard mentioned among some California tribes.

FROG
▼▼▼▼▼▼

"Cold. I am very cold," said Mole. "If I join my friends then maybe I can warm up." And so he went to visit Badger, cautiously walking through the dark that filled all of the earth at that time.

Squish, squish. Squish, squish. The earth was very soft and moist. Mole walked along with his feet squishing on the ground. Finally, he came to Badger's home, but he could not be sure since the world was so dark. "Badger, are you home?" he called. "Badger, I am here."

"Who is there?" asked Badger. "I cannot see you."

"Your friend Mole is here. I am cold and want to visit with you to warm up."

"Come in, come in, Mole, my friend," called Badger. "I am always pleased to see you." Feeling his way to the door, Mole walked in and followed the sound of Badger's voice to find a seat near his friend.

"How have you been, Badger?" asked Mole.

"I have been the same as always, just like our dark, wet, spongy earth. But I have news. A few days ago, a visitor came by who is making her way around the earth. She heard that above us in the sky there is another world. And that world has something called fire. They use this stuff called fire to give them warmth and light. It is powerful and, sometimes, dangerous, but it is a great help if you treat it with respect. This woman is calling everyone together in the hollow below the hill. She left me this string with knots tied in it. Every day when I get up from my sleep, I untie one knot. There are only two knots left and then we all need to gather and decide how we will get fire."

"Why, Badger, that is wonderful news. Maybe I will be warm after all. What can I do? I do not know where the sky is and I cannot see very well. Still, I will do whatever I can to help us get fire."

"That is good, Mole. You are very kind and a great friend. Stay with me for the next two days and we will go together."

Just then another voice called out.

"Badger, are you home? It is Otter, your friend. Have you heard the news? We are going to meet to decide how to get fire from the sky world."

"Come right in, Otter. Yes, we have heard the news. Mole is here with me and we will all go to the hollow when the time comes."

Otter asked, "Isn't it exciting? New worlds to explore and new friends to make. What a time we shall have."

"Indeed. It is always nice to see how other people live and to respect their customs. There are many different ways to live in this world, and, I suppose, in the sky world, too. When we explain our need for fire, I am sure those above us will want to help us out."

And so the three friends spent the next days talking about the coming adventure and staying warm in the company of each other. For meals and snacks they ate worms and bugs. For sleeping, they used giant leaves to roll up in, so Badger did not have to spend all of his time being a good host. After every sleep, another knot was untied.

On the second day, these three went to the hollow and met all of the other animal people. The woman who called them all together was Frog and she shouted to everyone there.

"I have heard that there is another world above us and that they have something called fire. It is very wonderful and very valuable. They keep it to themselves, but I do not think that they know about us. We will need to contact them and ask for a gift of fire. It can be divided up and so we will not deprive them of fire for their own needs. That should make those above willing to be generous with us."

"Good idea," said someone. "We are not greedy. We only want to make our world a better place than it is now. It is always a wet, cold night here. We should have more of a change."

"I want to be warm," said Mole. "I do not like to be cold all of the time. There must be a better way to live. My body tells me so."

"How shall we get there?" asked Badger. "I have only heard that the sky is above us, but I do not know how far it is or the way there. I want to help any way that I can."

Frog said, "I have asked Chickadee here with his mighty bow. He has volunteered to help us with his arrows."

"How can that be?" replied Mole. "Chickadee is so tiny and his bow is so large, how can he reach the sky?"

"Watch what you say, Mole," cautioned Otter. "You should not hurt Chickadee's feelings. Like you, he only wants to help us all."

"Oh, dear. I am sorry, Chickadee, if I insulted you. That was not my intent. I was only curious, and a bit skeptical, that you could shoot an arrow into the sky."

"Hmm. Well, then, I will show you, Mole," said Chickadee. "I have had lots of practice at shooting things far, far away. I have never hit the sky, though. Then again, I have never aimed for it, either. Now I will."

Thus saying, Chickadee took an arrow and nocked it into his bowstring. Pulling back the string as far as he could, he bent the bow into a C-shape and let go of the arrow. Everyone held their breath. They waited, and waited, and waited, and waited.

Some of them began to mutter, "Oh, see, he missed. The sky was too far away." Others continued to wait.

Some of the mutterers began to grumble, "Let us find our own way there. We'll beat up those sky people and take away their fire if we have to. We'll show them." Some of the crowd was shocked by such rude talk, but they kept silent and waited.

Finally, after a very long time, a sliver of light appeared far above their heads. It was like the tiny glow of a faded star. This weak glimmer appeared in the sky above them.

The crowd was hushed. "What is that?" everyone quietly asked a neighbor, for no one had ever seen such light before. It was a good thing that it was so tiny or everyone would have been overwhelmed.

"See, I told you I could reach the sky," cried out Chickadee. "Now I will do even better and I will shoot an arrow into the back of that first arrow and make a chain of arrows into the sky." With rapid fire, arrow after arrow, that is just what Chickadee did. Soon the last arrow was attached and the chain went from land to sky.

Then Frog spoke up. "Listen, everyone, we cannot all go into the sky to get fire. Only a few of us need go. We can travel more quickly that way, and hurry back with the fire. Who wants to go?"

Everyone spoke up and there was confusion. Again, Frog shouted, "Not everyone can go. Only the swiftest people can come along. That way we can make haste. Let me call out the names of likely travelers. Otter, you come. Snake, you come, too. And Flounder, come along. That will make four and that is a good number." Everyone agreed, and those four began to climb up.

The others watched and prayed until, from far in the back, they heard a rumble and a clanking. The crowd parted and there was Mrs. Bear, standing near the chain, loaded down with her pots and pans and packages.

"Let me through," she shouted. "Let me through. I want to get up into the sky and get my own fire. I want to set up my home in the sky. Everyone here is mean to me and gets in my way."

"No. No. You cannot do that, Mrs. Bear," the ones in front

pleaded. "You will hurt the chain and endanger our friends. We cannot let you go up."

But Mrs. Bear was very willful. She only cared for herself and her own family. The others could not stop her. They could only delay her climb.

"Please, Mrs. Bear," they said, "wait until the other four enter the sky world. Then you can climb up. We will not stop you if you only wait until the others are safe."

"It is not my nature to wait," said Mrs. Bear, "but since you ask nicely, I will wait until the others get into the sky world."

Since it took some time for all of this to happen, the crowd was again startled by a bigger and brighter flash of light from the sky as the first four made the hole bigger and disappeared. Never before had they seen light and now there was so much of it coming from the hole in the sky.

A moment later, Mrs. Bear with all of her belongings started up the arrow chain.

Up above, Frog and her friends had to stop and wait for their eyes to adjust to light. They were blinded by its very brightness and by the difference it made in the world. There was so much more to see and to ponder. Colors stood out everywhere, not just the shades of black and twilight they were used to seeing.

"I am overwhelmed," said Flounder. "How can we go on when there is so much to see just in this one spot? How can we take it all in and still keep moving?"

Frog took charge then. "Now, listen to me. All of this is new and different, but this world is like our own. Only here we can see better. Surely, since our eyes work here, something like this world was intended for us. By our own initiative, we will get fire and take it back to enable everyone to see what is around them and to better enjoy life. Come on, just set your mind to travel ahead and ignore most of what you see. That is the only way to keep going."

"But Frog," said Otter, "it is all so beautiful. I want to stay here until I have taken in all of this difference."

"Not me," added Snake. "I want to get going. Just sssstaying in one place getssss boring. Let'ssss go on ahead."

And so they did. They went on through green, grassy prairies and dark emerald forests. At the edge of the forest, they heard a noise.

"Hush. Quiet," whispered Frog. "Someone is near and we do not want to come upon them unannounced. Keep still. I will go ahead and spy on them. I will come back and report."

The other three nodded in agreement and Frog went on. She hid in the brush and crept close to the noise. Through branches she saw a person bigger than herself or any of her friends. The person was gathering old branches from the ground and piling them up.

Frog was afraid, but she took courage and slowly walked into the clearing, saying, "Hello there, we have come to ask for fire to light our world below."

Before the words were out of her mouth, the person looked shocked and screamed, "Mama, Mama, help. Someone strange is here. I'm scared, Mama."

Frog was herself surprised that this big person was only a child and tried to say, "Hush. Relax. I am a friend. I mean you no harm. I am sorry if I frightened you. We only came to ask for help."

At the same time, the earth began to shake and a rumbling filled the air. The sky darkened as a huge shape came closer, ever closer. It was taller than the trees they had to climb above to get into the sky. Suddenly, a giant woman stood in the clearing, deafening all other sounds. She shouted, "Leave my child alone, you nasty thing. He is too young to suffer such a fright. Go away where you belong and leave decent folks alone."

Frightened herself beyond measure, Frog croaked, "I am sorry. I come from the lower world where it is dark and wet and soft. We need fire to improve our world and keep us warm. I did not know your child was so young. I thought he was an adult like me, only bigger. Please help us."

"Who are you and how many of you are there? I see only yourself and you are smaller than our babies. How did you get here and why have you come? If you want to fight, you will lose because we are bigger and stronger than you, even if you are many. Just go back where you came from and forget about us."

"But we came for fire. We need fire. Can you help us?" said Frog. "We mean no harm. There are only four of us. Many others await us in the world below."

Mother and child now stood together. The child was safe and the mother was more calm. She listened to Frog.

"Fire. You want fire, did you say? Fire is a precious gift that requires much work and great care. It can be very dangerous if you ignore it. But it cooks things very well."

"What is this 'cook' you talk of?" asked Frog. "I do not know it."

"Oh, my, you poor thing. You do not know cooking. You truly do need help. Call your friends and I will take you home. I will wait here until you all come back." And she did as she said, while Frog went back into the forest.

"Snake, Otter, Flounder, come out. Where are you? I have made contact with a mother and child of the giants who live here. Come out."

There was no reply, so Frog went further into the forest, still calling to her friends. Uncertain where they had gone, she decided to stand in the place where she had left them and call some more. "Come out, please. We have been invited home with the giants. Come out."

Slowly and very, very quietly, Otter came out of the densest clump of bushes, whispering, "Frog, I'm so glad that you are still alive. When I heard the thumping and the yelling, I just knew that you were killed and gobbled up by some monster or other. Now the rumbling has stopped and you are here. Have you been tricked or sent back to trick us? Are we safe?"

"I think so," said Frog. "The giant woman is very large, but she is a kind mother to her child and seems to welcome strangers who can explain themselves. If we want fire, we will have to risk going with her. Where are the others? Are they near?"

Rustling bushes close by revealed that Flounder and Snake had regained confidence in Frog and were also willing to risk the visit to an unknown home.

As they went back to the clearing, Frog told the others that fire was used for something called "cooking" and they would learn about it when they got to the home of the giants.

The mother and child awaited them at the edge of the forest and Frog introduced her companions. "These are my friends: Otter, Flounder, and Snake. I am Frog. We came from far below to improve our dark and dripping world. You can help us, I am sure."

"Follow me," said the child. "Mama says that you are coming home with us to learn about cooking. I like to eat good cooking, but Mama never lets me go near the fire. She says it is too dangerous and I might get burned."

"Burned?" asked Frog. "What is burned? Is it like cooking?"

"You sure don't know a lot about stuff, do you?" replied the child. "Just wait until we get home and you'll learn all about cooking and burning."

Snake leaned over to Otter and whispered, "I do not like the ssssound of that. What do you think it meanssss? SSSShould we be frightened, or very cautioussss? Will we be hurt or killed?"

"Hush that," said Otter, very quietly. "These people offered to
help us. They are our hosts and we need to be respectful. If they
were going to harm us, they would have done so by now."

"Don't be sssso ssssure," continued Snake. "It will be easier to
do whatever they want with ussss once they get ussss home."

Flounder looked over at the whispering friends and gave them a
wondering look, but he did not say anything.

They continued on and soon a large house appeared in the distance.
The mother forged ahead to get to the door before the others.

"Hurry now," said the child. "We are almost home. Come to the
door and I will show you fire."

Amazed, the friends stood in the doorway and saw a flickering,
colorful something in a little cave along one wall. It moved and
changed with each moment. It rose and it fell in colors and forms
that were endlessly fascinating.

"That is fire," said the child. "Do not go too near or you will get
burned. Go up to it slowly so that you can feel the heat and warmth
in little bits. When it gets too hot, step back and you will be fine."

"Is it alive?" asked Frog. "Do you feed it and change it? Is it very
dangerous? How careful must we be?"

"It's not very alive," said the child. "It is easy to control because
you feed it wood from branches. The more you feed it, the bigger
it gets. If you want it to shrink, then you take some wood away or
you wait for the flames to die down."

"What are flames?" asked Frog, transfixed by the fire. "Are they
those tongue-like things that flicker all over?"

"Good for you. You got that right," said the mother. "Flames are
the parts of fire that reach out. You must be very careful of them
because they can burn you. Let me show you what fire can do to
help us."

From a nearby container, the mother took a piece of meat. "I will
cook this now for you to watch," she explained. She took a long rod
and pushed it through the meat and then hung it over the fire
between two forked braces. Slowly, the meat began to turn and the
flames licked it. A strange smell filled the room.

"Does the fire need to live in that cave?" asked Frog. "Do you
need to keep it in a small space so that it will cook whatever you
place near it?"

"Cave? How funny," said the mother. "This is called a fireplace
and it is specially made to hold the fire. You must do the same
below when you get home. Use rocks to build it and clay to cover

it so that a hard surface will bake onto the floor and walls. Make a hole into the sky because smoke must escape from a fire. If too much smoke stays near the fire, your eyes will hurt and get red."

"There is so much to learn!" said Frog.

"That is true and you better start now. Feed this branch to the fire," said the giant woman. "Be very careful and do not go too close. Be firm, but cautious. You must get the wood into the fire securely, but do not scatter the embers because their glowing can cause fires to start. When you leave, I will give you embers to take back and they will give you fire below. For now, you must practice respect for the fire."

Slowly, carefully, with sweaty palms, Frog moved toward the fire with a branch. "Oh, my. It is hot. The flames are bending toward me and the branch. I am going closer now. The flames are reaching for the wood. I can feel them. Here, fire, take this."

Wide-eyed, Snake, Otter, and Flounder looked on.

"Next time, each of you will take a turn feeding the fire. You too must learn how to be careful with fire," said the mother. "Look at the meat. See how it turns brown and feeds juices to the fire. It is cooking. If it cooks too long, it will blacken and that will mean that it burned. We cannot eat burned food. It does not taste good and it cannot feed us."

"Fire is sssso wonderful. Yet it sssseemssss sssso dangeroussss," remarked Snake.

"That is true," said the mother. "It can hurt your finger or hand. It can destroy this whole house. It can burn up an entire forest. You must respect it. It only does bad when you do not care for it. If you give it full attention, you will not be disappointed, hurt, or killed."

"How will we know when the meat is ready?" asked Flounder. "I am beginning to like the smell and the look of it."

"You are right," said the woman. "When it gets to be a warm brown and juicy, then it is ready. What do you eat below if you have no fire?"

"We eat thingssss assss we get them," said Snake. "We eat them assss they come. Wet, cold, plump, and sticky."

"I would not like your world," said the mother. "I like things clean, bright, warm, and juicy. Just like this meat. I'll bake some bread and then we will eat together. To get you ready, let me slice off some slivers of meat for you to eat as a snack so you will know what it tastes like."

She did so and gave a piece to each of them.

Gingerly, each held the bite while it cooled, watching it in their fingers. Frog took the first nibble and said, "This is good. It tastes firm and grainy. It is not like the mushy things we eat below. I like it."

"Me, too," said Otter. "Me, three," said Flounder. "Me, four," said Snake.

"But this is the way this always tastes," said the child. "You make it sound wonderful, but it is ordinary."

"Only for you, my child," said the mother. "Other people have other ways, and all of them are good. You may not like their food or houses, but you should not insult them for living their own way."

"Thank you," said Frog. "We will remember your advice all of our lives if we get back to the world below."

"Oh, yes. I should feed you so that you can carry fire back. Let me set out bowls and I will bake the bread and cut the meat."

Just then, there was a deafening noise. Crash! Bash! Shudder! Thud! Splat!

Everyone froze where they were.

After a time, Frog asked, "What was that?"

"I do not know," answered the mother. "Things are fine here. The sounds came from way off. There is nothing there that I know of. Do you?"

"That is the direction that we came from," said Otter and Frog. "Something must have happened to our ladder. Oh, no. Let us find out quickly."

Back they ran to the hole in the sky where they had crawled out. The giant mother was careful to hold her child, saying, "Do not go too close. It is a long way down, and you would not like what you found there, if you survived."

Frog went to the hole and looked down. "I see far below that Mrs. Bear has tumbled down from our arrow chain. She broke it. All of her pots and bundles were too heavy. It was just like her to try to take everything with her. Now, what are we to do? We have fire from our friends, but nowhere to take it."

Sadness descended on the group. They were alone.

"I want to go home," pleaded Flounder. "I cannot stay here. I do not know where the water is. I can see a patch of it far below. If I jump there, I will be safe."

Before the others could react, they saw Flounder jump through the hole.

Otter looked down and described what he saw. "Flounder has his arms and legs way out and he is floating down at a rapid speed. I do not think that he is aiming at water. I think it is a meadow. He is getting closer, closer, closer."

Splat! was the sound the friends heard. Flounder had indeed landed in a boggy meadow and so he was not killed. But he landed so hard that he was flattened. After he came to, he dragged himself into nearby water and slowly swam to the sea. That is why flounders still live on the bottom of the sea and are very flat fish.

Snake was looking down and cried out, "SSSSee, Flounder issss moving away from where he landed. He lookssss well. I'm going to follow him down." And so saying, Snake jumped.

"Oh, no, Snake. It is not safe!" screamed Frog, but it was too late. "Snake has his hands and feet together. If only he will dive. Then he might survive."

As if hearing, that is just what Snake did. He made his body long and thin. He was lucky to land, not in the marsh, but in a pond, but the impact on his body was so great that he was forever changed. He became long and thin. He lost the use of his arms and legs. He had to crawl from then on.

Frog looked at Otter and said, "Do not try the same thing. It is not safe. Wait here in the sky until we decide how we will return."

Dismayed, the mother and child stood looking. Finally, the mother spoke. "Do not despair, either of you. Come back to the house and I will give you fire and food for the return journey."

Frog and Otter followed her home. The child was silent during the walk. When they got home, however, the child went to his toys and said, "See, here, I have a kite. I will give it to you and you can use it to float back below."

"That is a good idea," said the mother. "You just have to be careful to guide the kite to the place where you want to land. Otherwise, you will be blown far from your home."

"It sounds dangerous, but we will try it," decided Frog. Otter was less sure, but he said, "If you think it will work, let's try it. I do not want to jump and hurt myself. I am not sure that it will work, though."

The mother took embers from the fire and wrapped them up with a bit of wood inside a clay pot. She gave them to Frog, who said, "Thank you, very much. You have made our world a better place. Now all we have to do is to get the fire home."

Otter took the kite and Frog took the pot and they went back to the edge of the hole. As they looked down, Otter said, "I will hold the kite string and Frog will hold on to me."

Frog agreed so that she would be able to hold the fire. When she tried to hold on to Otter and the pot at the same time, she realized that that would not work. "Otter," said Frog, "I need to hold on to you, but I cannot also hold the pot. Instead I will put the pot in my mouth and hold on to you." When she put the pot in her mouth, it stretched and so frogs now have large mouths.

Otter wrapped the string around his arms and waist and eased the kite through the hole. Frog rode on his back. After a first jolt, the kite hovered in the air and carried the friends away from the sky. They fell to the lower world at a steady, but not rapid, pace.

Otter learned to control the movement of the kite during the descent, explaining to Frog, "See, by pulling on the strings tied to the sides of the kite, I can make us go back home." As they got ever closer to their home, it got darker and darker. Otter could not see the ground well. He misjudged the distance, and the pair crashed into the top of a tall tree. Its branches and leaves tried to break their fall because the Tree knew of their mission. Otter was saved by the growth, but Frog was pitched off. She fell to the ground.

When she tried to scream on the way down, the pot burst from her mouth and broke on the earth. Flames began to flicker in the grass and soon rose into the trees. Fire spread over the world and would have done great damage except that everyone was waiting for it.

Flounder and Snake had prepared them. Every time a flame arose, someone took it and put it in a pot or bowl and took it home. Fireplaces had been prepared and their clay coverings began to bake. Soon, fire was contained, but it retained the possibility of rampaging over the landscape if people got careless.

Frog landed headfirst and was changed forever. Her arms were shoved up and shortened and her back was bent. Thereafter, frogs have had to hop because of their short arms and long legs. Their bulging eyes and wide mouths are proof of the time that Frog carried fire back to the people.[7]

DOG
▼▼▼▼▼▼▼

"I'm hungry," said the child. "I have not had food in days and this thin soup will not fill me up. Will we ever have real food again?"

"Hush, my child," answered the mother. "We have famine and

all of the families in our village are starving. All of us are starving and losing weight, except the Buzzards who live at the edge of the settlement. We do not know what they eat, but it is probably nasty. Eat what we have, please, and eventually we will have food again. Just take your time."

When the child finished drinking the soup, she said, "I am going to spy on that old Buzzard couple and find out what they are eating." The child watched and waited in secret, but all she could ever say to her mother was, "The old man Buzzard went for long walks and the old woman Buzzard stayed home and cooked over a small fire."

Finally, the mother and other adults met to decide how to spy on the Buzzards. "What shall we do?" they asked one another. "Will someone come forward to solve this quandary?"

They debated for some time until Dog spoke up. "I will volunteer to undertake this task. I will turn myself into a small pet and manage to get myself adopted into the household of these Buzzards. I will watch them carefully and I will report back to you the outcome."

Dog took the form of the modern animal. He was small, hairy, and cute. He stood by the trail near the Buzzards' home and waited. When the old woman went to get water, Dog made himself look hurt and bedraggled.

"Oh, look at the cute puppy," Buzzard woman muttered to herself. "He needs help and care. I have no children at home and my husband is often away. He could keep me company. I am talking this way so as not to scare this little one. He needs to get used to my voice. That way he might follow me home and I can offer him food as an enticement."

"You do that," thought Dog. "This will be easier than I realized. All I have to do is look woebegone and follow her at a safe distance. This should work."

"I will go on and get water and then give some to this dog. That way he will get used to me," said the woman. And that is what she did.

"Come on home with me, puppy," the woman coaxed. The Dog followed, as if begrudgingly. At the door of the lodge, the woman stood and said, "Do not run away, doggy. I am going to get you a treat. Stay near."

Acting wise, as though he understood her words (which he did), the Dog stayed at the edge of the yard. He could hear the woman rummaging around inside, moving bundles and packs until there was a pause and a rustling. Soon she came out. "Here you are, puppy. Try this. If this does not make you want to live here, nothing will," said Buzzard lady.

Suspiciously, Dog sniffed and moved forward, pondering. "This old woman is offering me a piece of meat. I have not had meat in weeks. Truly she is powerful, or her husband is. Maybe they both are. How can this be? Now I really am curious about their abilities. How can they have meat? If I move into the house with them, I should be able to find out."

For their own reasons, Buzzard and Dog came together. Dog stayed in one place and allowed the woman to pet him. Soon he rolled over and was content. So was the woman. Now she had a pet and companion. They were happy together.

Until the husband came home, that is. They heard him coming and the woman said, "That is my husband. He is often away, so you, puppy, will help keep me company. I will explain that to him, but he may not listen. He is very stubborn and opinionated. Let me deal with him." By then, the husband was inside the door.

"What is this runt thing?" he shouted. "I go away and get us food, and you take in strays. Have you no sense, wife? He may be a spy. Where did he come from and how did he get here? Can you tell me that? No, don't bother. Out he goes. Go away, mutt. Shoo."

Dog cringed and thought quickly. "If I look harmless and cower, that should help. This husband, Buzzard old man, is a smart one. I will have to be very careful and act even more like a pet. If I crouch beside the woman, that might help. Let me do that." And he did.

"Leave him alone," the wife shouted at the husband. "He is only a puppy and can do us no harm. I like him and want him for a pet. You are away so much of the time, he can keep me company. Let him stay. He is harmless. He can cause no trouble. I will care for him."

After this stiff defense, the husband relented. "Oh, well, if you insist. The dog can stay, but I am still very suspicious. We need to watch him at all times. If need be, we will tie him up so he cannot go too far or try to follow me. Is that agreed?"

"Yes, indeed," the woman agreed and Dog, ever watchful, stayed the night in the lodge with the old Buzzard couple.

The next morning, the husband got up and said to his wife, "I am still dubious about this dog. Let us test him. Give him meat. If he gobbles it up, we will know he is a real dog. If he eats it slowly, we will know he is an imposter."

The Dog, of course, heard this and gobbled the food placed in front of him.

"Well, he looks and acts like a dog, but I am still not sure," said the husband as he left the lodge for the day. Dog stayed close to the woman and kept her company. She grew to like Dog even more.

At dusk, the Buzzard man returned with fresh meat hidden under his cloak, gave it to the woman, and rested while she cooked it. "How was the dog today?" he asked. "Did he act like a dog? Did he leave your sight? Was he overly curious?"

"He was a good dog, friendly and close by. He was very much a dog. Do not worry," responded the wife.

"We must be careful," warned the husband. "Tomorrow I will need your help because the herd needs to be culled. It is getting much too large for the space. I will leave in the morning and you will join me at noon. Pretend that you are going for water. Make sure to tie up the dog. Then meet me at the place."

"I will do as you say. What if the dog howls? I cannot leave him unattended or someone will come by to find out what is going on," explained the wife.

"Just leave him food and water, and he will be fine," ordered the old Buzzard.

Hearing all this, Dog decided to be quiet when the woman left so that he could follow her. Then everyone went to sleep.

At dawn the next day, the husband rose and said, "I am still not sure of this dog, let me grab his tail and see what he will do." When his tail was grabbed, Dog yelped and then bared his teeth, but he did not growl.

"Well," said the husband. "He certainly acts like a dog. He growls but does not snap. He knows who feeds him and shows proper respect. But I am still not sure."

"You have much to do today," replied the wife. "Why do you waste your time with the dog? Get going. It will be a long day."

"You are right," Buzzard man responded. "There is much to do and I feel the burden of it. I had best be on my way."

During the morning, the old woman puttered around the home, getting straps and bundles together to take with her. Later, she led the dog outside and tied him to one of the lodge supports, leaving food and water for him.

Then she left.

While the rope was being tied, Dog puffed up his neck so that what had been a firm knot to the woman came loose after she left and Dog exhaled. He also wished himself smaller so he could slip out of the noose and follow Buzzard woman along the shadowy edge of the trail she took.

After she started across country, Dog stayed behind her in the darkness of the undergrowth. She went toward a hillside deep in the forest.

As they approached, Dog saw the old man sitting in the sun beside an opening in the rocky surface of the hill.

"So," he said. "You have come. Did you bring everything?"

With a chuckle, the woman replied, "Of course I did. Every time we do this, you ask the same question and I give you the same answer."

Together, the couple cut saplings and formed them into a drying rack. When it was finished, the man went to a flat rock just inside the opening of the cave. He lifted one side ever so slightly and a buffalo squeezed out and stood before him.

"Thank you for coming out," the old man prayed. "We need food and wish you to die that we may eat. Please do so now and we will add your bones to the pile and you will be reborn below."

The bison rolled on its side and died. Buzzard woman came up to it and placed her hand on its shoulder. "Thank you" was all that she said. Then she cut the meat into thin strips and hung them on the drying frame, praying, "We do not have much time. Please dry quickly."

The strips turned brown and began to dry. They became quite light and easy to carry.

Dog watched as the man repeatedly lifted the rock and prayed to each emerging buffalo. The woman prepared them for drying. After a short time, Dog thought, "Now I know their secret. I will go home and wait for them." And he did so. When he got there he wished himself normal size after the rope loop was again around his neck.

At dusk the couple returned, very, very tired.

Still, the woman took the time to untie the dog and say, "See, old man, you have nothing to worry about. My pet has been here all day. He moved with the sun and stayed in the shade. His food is gone and most of his water."

Following the Buzzards inside, Dog watched as they shook tiny bags from their outer garments and spaced them along the inside walls. The old man prayed, "Now you are home. Grow to your full size and keep us fed for a while." And that is what the bags did. They were full of dried meat and filled the lodge.

Dog was amazed and afraid because of the awesome power displayed by the Buzzards. "I must be very careful," he thought. "I must not make them suspicious. I will stay two more days to fool them and then I will take action."

During the next two days, however, Dog sometimes lost his resolve. "I am very well fed and I have only to be friendly to stay that way. Why should I endanger myself for others? They should be able to take care of themselves."

At other times, Dog thought, "I can hear babies and children crying from hunger even now. Someone should help them, but only I know what to do. The more I live with the Buzzards the more dirty I know them to be. They leave uneaten food all over inside the lodge. It goes bad and smells, but, even so, they will not share it with others. They are selfish. They think only of themselves. I will save the people."

Back and forth, Dog had such thoughts. On the morning of the fifth day, he was still undecided. He had grown attached to the woman and the man. But that morning the man behaved badly. When Dog went to nuzzle him, Buzzard man kicked him and called out, "Get away from me, you cur. All you do is eat my food and take my wife's affection from me. She wants you here, so you must stay, but keep away from me."

"I will do it now," thought Dog. "I will not put up with cruelty. I will teach him a lesson, and her, too." Dog cowered in a corner and waited for the man to leave. The woman tried to soothe her pet, but he whined until she let him out of the lodge. He went off into the nearby bushes and curled up. The woman let him be, and went about the task of tanning the buffalo hides she brought back. When she began to rub rotted brains into the skins to soften them, Dog moved further away.

"Strange. Very strange," mumbled the old woman. "Usually dogs like this rotting smell, yet my own dog is being fastidious. How can this be?" Thus musing, she continued her work, and soon became preoccupied with it.

"Now is my chance," thought Dog. "I will sneak away, but just to be sure, I will wish a dummy here to take my place." As he moved further away into the brush, a likeness of himself materialized to look like a curled-up dog.

Dog went directly to the cave, approaching cautiously. Old man Buzzard was nowhere to be seen. He was far away. Dog crept up to the rock, changed back into his human shape, and lifted the cover away from the opening. Instantly, the ground shook and the air filled with the sound of thunder. Bison escaped and filled the landscape. They went everywhere, but only reached the place where the man was an hour or so later.

Flabbergasted, Buzzard man screamed, "Where are these buffalo coming from? I have the only ones and they are locked up. Can these be mine?" And he rushed to the cavern, but by then all of the bison were long gone.

As he got closer and heard no sound, he relaxed more and more, thinking, "Those must be someone else's buffalo. Mine are still here. I could see and hear them, otherwise."

But when he stood before the cave and saw the stone upturned and the hole vacant, he screamed and cried. "That dog. It must have been that dog. Now we are destitute. We will have no food." Sobbing, he picked himself up and went home.

His wife knew nothing of their loss. She had heard the rumbling, but the bison had stayed away from the village. They did not like the smell of people. They went out onto the plains and grazed in the sunlight. They rolled in the dust and dirt until their damp hair dried and they got used to the freedom of the vast expanse of grasslands.

From far away, Buzzard woman heard wailing. As it came closer, she recognized the sound of her husband's voice, saying, "Wife, wife, we are undone. The dog tricked us and has stolen our game."

She looked over to where the dog was sleeping and watched it fade before her eyes. Then she too knew the truth, and began to wail. "How could I have been so stupid? I was lonely and wanted company. Was that so bad? Was it just bad luck, or do I deserve this?" She collapsed and cried. There was no more food for her or her husband.

The old man fell down beside his wife and he, too, cried.

The village was startled by this uproar, but no one came to their aid. The elders were even then meeting with Dog, who explained what he had learned and what he had done with that knowledge.

"It will not be easy, you understand," Dog told them. "Buffalo are scattered all over the place. You will have to hunt them, sometimes for days. They are intelligent beings. Even when they were captives, Buzzard had to pray to them and respect their lives. You will need to do the same. They will not allow themselves to be killed for nothing. You must explain your needs to them. You must ask them for meat. You must use all of the parts that you can. Make thread of the sinews, tools of the bones and horns, and clothing of the robes. Leave the offal for other people, who will also need to live."

"We will do that," agreed the elders. "It is good. We will respect the buffalo who give us life. But what of the Buzzards? They owned the bison, and now they have lost them. How will they live? It is true that in the past, they thought only of themselves. But we must not be as unkind as they were. We must teach them a lesson."

Dog responded, "I have given this much thought. Buzzards will hereafter become birds that live on offal. They will like the stink and rot, just as they have done until now. But they will live away from people and help keep the land clean. They will have an easy life because other beings will always die and buzzards will live off of them."

And so it has become.[8]

SWANS
▼▼▼▼▼▼

"What a fine day," Coyote said aloud. "I think I will go to visit those Swan brothers with the pretty sister." And so he prepared to do so.

Knowing that the Swans would recognize him on sight and suspect trickery, Coyote wished for a disguise. "I want a beautiful buckskin outfit, a headband of white weasel skin, and a handsome face and form." Because of his power, what Coyote wished for was granted. He changed into a handsome man of the Arrow Lakes tribe and went off on his visit.

The five brothers were away during the day, hunting up food. Their Swan sister was home alone, and offered hospitality to the visitor. "Will you have some food?" she asked.

Coyote did not reply, in a haughty but respectful way. When she put the food in front of him, he pushed it away and acted stern. He implied by this action that he was an important man who would wait for proper attention. The sister went quietly about her work.

When the brothers arrived home, the sister said, "This important man wants to see you." All of the brothers were impressed by their visitor's pride, except for the youngest brother, who said, "I think this man looks a lot like Coyote and even smells like him." The others said, "Be quiet, he is our guest." After chatting and eating, everyone was even more impressed by the fine talk and manners of the stranger.

The brothers took their sister aside and said, "Here is a fine man for you to marry. He is important and rich and dresses well." Thus urged by her brothers, the sister married the disguised Coyote and made room for him on her side of the mat lodge she shared with her family.

During the day, the brothers hunted in the highest mountains around Arrow Lakes because animals there were prized for their firm and ample meat.

After a few days of married life, the new husband asked, "Can I go with you?" The youngest brother said, "No way," but the older ones consented. The oldest brother said, "I will carry you, brother-in-law, but I will have to leave you on the shore of a lake because the mountains are too high for me to carry you up to where we hunt." The husband agreed.

They flew away and left Coyote by the lake. In a short time, when the brothers were well out of sight, Coyote said, "I want to be myself and change back." After he did, he then took a driftwood tree and began to pound on the ground. Moles came out of their holes and Coyote clubbed them. He singed their bodies in a fire and gobbled them up. Moles were his favorite food, although everyone else thought that eating them was disgusting. He ate his fill.

"Honk, honk, honk, honk, honk," the Swans called from a long way off. "I want all trace of my fire to disappear and I want to be changed back into a Lakes man," Coyote said. The brothers slowly spiraled down from the peaks to the beach, where their brother-in-law stood.

"Did you have a good day?" the brothers asked.

"I had a fine day enjoying this remote place and its scenery," the Lakes man responded.

"Let's go home," said the brothers. And the older ones added, "We will carry you." The youngest brother only grumbled quietly, "We should leave him here. I warn you."

For the next several days, everyone stayed close to home and rested. After a while, everyone said, "Let's get some fresh meat in the mountains," and the men went back to the lakes, leaving their brother-in-law on the beach. For months, this routine continued, only the youngest brother grumbled more and more, "We are being taken advantage of by this freeloader."

Indeed, while the brother-in-law told wonderful stories and entertained during long meals, all he did was eat up what everyone else provided. "I will do something about this the next time we go into the mountains," the youngest brother promised himself.

Eventually the older brothers said, "We need fresh meat and a change of climate. Let's go into the mountains and take our brother-in-law." They did so.

Left on the shore, Coyote wished, "I want to change back into myself" and he did. He took his tree trunk and pounded on the ground, forcing moles out of their burrows. He killed them, rolled their bodies in the fire to burn off the hair, and gobbled them up. "Yum. Yum. Moles are delicious," he sighed and was content. He lost track of everything else in his revelry.

Meanwhile, the youngest brother was telling his brothers, "Why don't you realize that our brother-in-law is really Coyote and he is taking advantage of us? Aren't you tired of carrying him up here all the time? What does he do for us in return?"

"What the youngest says is mostly true," another brother agreed, and soon they all did. The oldest one, who best liked the stranger, said, "Let's be absolutely sure about this first. Let's glide down to the beach and spy on the Lakes man and see what he does when we are up here hunting in the peaks."

They did so and saw the truth. Silently, they flew back to a mountain top. When they landed, they cried out in unison, "Yetch. That man is Coyote and he is eating disgusting moles. Lots and lots of moles. We were tricked. Now we will fix him." They decided on a plan.

"Honk. Honk. Honk. Honk. Honk." The Swans called from a distance and Coyote hurried to say, "I want to be changed back into a handsome Lakes man and have all trace of my fire and meal disappear." This happened.

When they landed, the eldest brother said, "Come. We are ready to go home. Get on my back." Coyote did so. Up. Up. Up. Up. They flew high into the sky, but instead of heading to the lowlands, they flew over the lake. When they got to the center, the eldest dropped Coyote and he fell. Down. Down. Down. Down. Splash. Deeper and deeper he went.

"I want to be bone, a thin, light bone to float on the water," Coyote wished with all his might. But when he opened his mouth to say the words, water rushed in and all he could exclaim was, "I want to be a s-t-o-n-e" and so he was and sunk to the very bottom of the very, very deep lake.

When things settled, fish and water bugs gathered to see. "What is this?" they asked each other. Suddenly, the stone spoke. "Help me, I am Coyote and I lost my way. Help me out and I will grant any wish that you have for me."

The water creatures jabbered among themselves. "Coyote never tells the truth. If we help him, we will only end up tricked. Let's go away and leave him be. Then everything will be fine."

"Noooo. Don't do that," Coyote pleaded. "If you help me, I will help you. Maybe you want to be more pretty or bigger or more impressive. I can do that for you. Just get me out of here and I will do it. My power only works in the air. It is not for water."

Now the water creatures knew that Coyote really did need their help because his power could not help him at all. A big salmon said, "Coyote, you had better be telling the truth. I will help you and so will the others. I will put you in my mouth and swim near the shore to drop you." A bunch of little fish added, "Coyote, we will push you toward the land from the shallows." Finally, water bugs agreed, "Coyote, we will roll you all the way to the land. Then we will all ask for what we want to be granted."

"Wonderful. Do it," cried Coyote.

And they did, but before all the water beings could gather around the landed rock, Coyote shouted, "Change me back into the fastest Coyote of all time," and he zoomed off over the hills.

"Wait. Wait. Coyote, wait," all the fishes and bugs shouted. "You promised to give us what we asked for."

From far away, carried on the wind, the water animals heard only these faint words from Coyote, "I don't have time to lounge around while you make up your minds. I have many things to do and no time to waste. If you could not ask when I was ready, you will never be ready to do so at all."[9]

NAMER AND SHAPER
▼▼▼▼▼▼▼

"Humans are coming soon and the world has to be made ready for them," the Spirit Chief constantly reminded everyone else. "You will need to decide what you will be and what you will do. Most of you will help, but some will become monsters. It is up to you to decide. Shaper and Namer will be my specially appointed agents. They will make most things ready for humans."

"Who is this Shaper?" someone asked the Spirit.

"He is named 'The One from Down Under' because he was born in the water. His father is White Stone, his mother is Young Doe, and his nephew is Duck. He has many relatives. He wears clothes painted red and casts a red shadow. I gave him the ability to trick certain immortals who were hoarding resources so these can be scattered around the world for human use. He has already done this with many fruits, with flint, and with evergreens."

"And who is Namer?" another person asked.

"Namer crawls over the earth on his hands and knees, leaving streams and rivers in his wake. His job is to provide names for everything. You will know when humans are near because Namer will have finished his task."

"We will watch for it," the friendly spirits responded.

Indeed, that day came shortly after. As people watched from afar, Namer stood up to stretch and stuck his head on the sky, knocking off his feathered hat. As it fell to the ground, Namer uttered his last words, "The place where my hat lands will be called Ear." The long, low hill marking his last resting place can still be seen on Canal Flats, British Columbia.

As Namer transformed, the Spirit knew that all was in readiness. He called an immediate council of the immortals, saying, "Gather around, all of you. You must now decide the form you will take, the place where you will live, and how you will regard humans."

Most responded with helpful decisions, such as Deer, who said, "I will become a quiet animal with much meat. Humans will hunt me and live off my flesh. As long as they respect me and thank me, I will come to them and offer my flesh." Frog said, "I will guard the water and I will be grandmother to everyone. I will live in a pond on Tobacco Plains and I will send offspring to other watery homes."

As the first humans began to emerge from water, Rabbit made the last decision. "I will be a small, hopping, and inoffensive being. People will hunt me for my fur and for my meat."

The Chief Spirit had made humans from either the blood or the hairs of a giant bear who had been swallowed by a water monster. He made so many humans because he wanted them to fill the earth.

The Kootenay and the Shaper lived together for some time, but the tribe grew fearful of his power. He threatened them and their women, so the Kootenay killed him, and threw his body into the water.

As he rested on the bottom, Shaper called to the fish, "Come restore me. The water is my home and I will come back to life to get revenge." The fish gathered around and chanted. Soon, the body came back to life. He swam to the surface and walked to the nearest camp. When Shaper got there he bellowed, "You had no faith in me. You abused me. Now you will die." And they did.

After Shaper had punished the people, he left, saying, "There is much more to the world than this place. I will go to visit all of it. I will travel for the rest of my life."[10]

LIZARD
▼▼▼▼▼▼

"Human beings are coming soon, and we should decide which of our own advantages should be shared with humans." Lizard, Eagle, and Bear were deep in discussion about their relative abilities.

"I fly high above the earth and see everything that happens," said Eagle. "When I see food on the run or swimming in the water, I pounce on it from far above. Humans should be like me."

"No," said Bear. "That would not be right. Humans would need feathers and sharp beaks. We all know that humans will be weak creatures with nothing special to help them except their wits. They will have to walk on the ground and eat the sorts of berries and fruits that I do. I will share my wild foods with humans."

"I like that idea," said Lizard. "But humans should walk upright on two legs so that they can gather these foods."

"I push the branches to me with my paws and pull the berries off with my teeth," said Bear. "Humans can do like me."

"Oh no, food should not have to move or be handled in a clumsy way," said Eagle. "I eat my fish or meat after it is dead on the ground. That is what humans should do, too."

"No. This is inappropriate. Humans will have to move all over and eat when they can. They will need to hide in the woods like I do," argued Lizard. "They will need help gathering food so that they can pack it along while they travel. Humans will need hands like mine. They will need a thumb and fingers to grasp and pick and hold. I will give them hands like lizards, Bear will show them how to eat berries and nuts, and Eagle will teach them to enjoy meat."

Bear and Eagle thought about this.

Eagle said, "I like my claws, but I can see where people as helpless as humans would be inconvenienced if they had to walk around and handle things with claws at the ends of their fingers and toes."

Bear agreed. "My paws work for me because I walk on all four legs, but if humans only have two legs and two arms, then Lizard is right about how their hands should be formed."

It was decided. Humans would have hands like Lizard.

Eagle then offered, "I will also give humans keen sight since they will not be able to use my claws or beak to kill game." The others agreed.

As a result of their discussion, Eagle, Bear, and Lizard decided, "When they arrive, humans will have two hands, each with five fingers. They will have keen eyes, and eat a mixture of meat and fruit." And so it came to pass.[11]

PART THREE

SHAPING ANIMALS

▼▼▼▼▼▼▼▼▼▼▼

The Animal People of yore become more and more like the members of their species in this period. Decisions are made and deeds are done that establish quite specific patterns and behaviors. What is lost in terms of supernatural talents or abilities is made up for by the fellowship of other creatures. No longer are spirit and species combined in a single form. Spirits now become separate from animals and plants, but they continue to share and talk to each other. Humans are also becoming more evident on the landscape, at least in some regions.

Salmon, the staple food among tribes of the northern Pacific drainage, was liberated by Coyote. The events occur on the modern border between the states of Washington and Oregon, but their consequences were timeless until dam construction and pollution have brought this majestic fish to the brink of extinction. Coyote again works from selfish motives, but people are willing to compromise with him in different ways along the villages at the mouths of Columbia River tributaries.

Species peculiarities, learned with anatomical precision by hunters respectfully butchering their catch, are the subject of many stories. Here the lack of gall bladder or of dew claws has its origins in a friendly encounter. The environmental life styles of Antelope and Deer also figure in this version.

Spider is a being of great power throughout the Americas. Often the flow of power through the universe is phrased in terms of the spokes and rings of a spider web. The intersections are places of great energy, and the center is the site of the village or home of the narrator. Among the Lakota or Sioux tribes, Iktomi as Spider is a complex figure of good and bad, of reaction and misadventure. His profound innocence or stupidity often gets featured treatment.

Loon woman is an important character in a set of linked stories from northern California tribes. Her actions tell much about the dangers of sibling rivalry or incest. By her errors and terrors, set against the good deeds of her brother, family life was given a model to emulate forever afterward.

The elaborate social and town life of the Northwest Coast tribes was based in a series of separate households. Like royal houses, these plank-covered buildings sheltered people who recounted the adventures of their ancestors so they could be remembered and extolled. Their names, actions, and locations became inherited property from each generation to the next. While all tribes have stories about encounters with Bears, among the Tsimshian and other coastal tribes social patterns already existing were given color and meaning by such particular incidents.

For Pueblos of the Southwest, the Turkey was a being of great wisdom, kindness, and insight. Aside from the dog, the turkey was the only other domesticated animal in North America. South America had the llama, vicuña, and alpaca, along with the guinea pig; but North America had only the dog and this bird, who became a symbol of Thanksgiving. As described in this story, turkeys have been kept in pens in these towns for a thousand years at least. Similarly, tales of orphans who make good are also widely distributed throughout the Americas, indicating that they have long been a concern of Native communities.

SALMON
▼▼▼▼▼

"It is dinner time. Time to take salmon from our personal fishtrap. Time to enjoy our own special food," said the youngest of the five sisters who lived together near the mouth of the Columbia River.

"Good idea," agreed the others. "You go down and bring up a salmon while we get the rest of the food assembled for our meal."

And the youngest sister did so.

When she returned with the clubbed salmon, the other sisters had put out cooked roots, fresh vegetables, and berries for the meal. The salmon was boiled and all ate from the same kettle. Afterwards, all of the bones were gathered up and placed back into the fishtrap set in the river. As soon as the bones hit the bottom, they turned back into a salmon. If any bones were lost, the salmon was crippled until the bones were found and added to the water.

These sisters were shore birds and they enjoyed the only access to salmon in the world at that time. During the day, they scattered out along the plains and dug roots, picked greens, or gathered fruits. In the fall, they harvested many kinds of berries.

They lived well and were content. If strangers came by they were made to feel unwelcome. The sisters did not want to share the secret of the salmon. Yet word had leaked out that these women had something special. Eventually Coyote heard about it.

Coyote was greedy, selfish, and powerful. At the beginning of the world, he was the first creature to think for himself and so was given particular powers by the Creator. Unlike other beings, whose center was their heart, Coyote's power was in his intestines. When he needed help, he called to his "little sisters" who came out and spoke to him.

"Come out, come out, my little sisters," Coyote said as he squatted down. Reluctantly, the sisters came out.

"What do you want, Coyote?" they responded. "You always ask for our help and when we give it, you always say that you knew it all along and that we were no help to you. But we know that we do help you, regardless of what you say."

"Quiet, little ones," ordered Coyote. "If you will not be silent, I will call the rain to wash you away. Be careful and pay attention. I need to ask you something."

"We will listen," they gurgled.

"I hear that there are some lovely women down the big river and that they have a special food, a very tasty food. They will not allow anyone to visit them. They will not share. They are bad women and no one has been able to get the better of them. What should I do to trick them out of that special food?"

The sisters stood for a moment and then said, "Coyote, you will have to change yourself. Anyone who knows of or about you will know your ways and send you packing. You will not have a chance. You must look innocent and harmless. You must become a baby. Those women would probably fuss over a baby. That will be how you will trick them."

"No, sisters," shouted Coyote, "that will not work. I am too old to be a baby and I do not like messy diapers. I am strong and clean."

"You are mangy and hardly strong," replied the sisters. "Squat down so that we can get back inside. We have had enough. Either follow our advice or fail. Those are your only choices."

Coyote let the sisters return, and he went on his way. After some time, he said aloud, "My sisters are no help. I will have to rely on my own cleverness. I will turn into a baby. That is something they did not think of. I will be bound in a cradleboard that will float down the river."

And saying so, he did so. He became a baby laced into a large wooden cradleboard and floated down the Columbia. After a time, he lodged against the fishtrap owned by the sisters. When the oldest went to get a salmon for their meal, she rushed back to their home, shouting, "Sisters, sisters, come quick. I have found a baby. A cute little baby. Abandoned and resting on the water against our trap. He will be ours."

"What is this about a baby? How do you know it is a boy? All I see is a soggy lump of wood and leather," said a middle sister.

"That is a mighty suspicious baby," questioned the youngest. "Look at his eyes, they are much too alert for any ordinary baby. It is some monster or someone else trying to trick us. Throw it back into the river and sink it."

"No. No, he is now mine," argued the oldest sister. "He has the cradleboard of a boy. That is how I know he is a boy. He is bright and intelligent to survive in the water for so long. That is why his eyes look as they do. Soon I will change him and make him dry, then we will know for sure. If you do not want him, I do. If you will not help to care for him, then I will do it alone."

"No, sister," said the others, "that is not right. We are a family and we will all help be mothers."

"I will help, too, but I remain suspicious," cautioned the youngest. "For now, though, we must be kind and keep the baby warm and dry."

They all helped to change and clean the baby. They all admired his strong limbs and tiny body.

"Look, he has teeth," said the oldest. "He does not seem old enough to have teeth. He is truly advanced in growth and intelligence. Look how he watches us. Let us feed him bits of our food. Otherwise we will have to use salmon broth to feed him."

"Slowly, he eats our food," whispered a sister. "He will be easy to care for. He can eat solid food. He will be a very good boy."

Thus pleased with their new responsibility, the sisters retired for the night, leaving the baby in a warm, dry cradle. Coyote wished that the trick was over so that he could share beds with these sisters, but he knew that would defeat his plan and, for once, he restrained himself. Still, he thought, "That salmon stuff is very good. Roasted or broiled, it tastes wonderful. I can hardly wait to eat a whole fish by myself. These little morsels do me no good. I am a big man and I must eat in quantity to sustain myself. Tomorrow I will begin the work of freeing the salmon." With that he went to sleep.

In the morning, the sisters continued their discussions.

"I want to take the baby with me today," said the oldest.

"No, you can't do that, I want to take the baby with me," said another.

"Neither of you can because I will take the baby with me," responded a third.

The youngest took charge, saying, "No. No one will take the baby with them as they wander over the plains. It will slow you down. We will get less food. We will leave the baby laced in his cradle and suspended from this tree. He will rock in the wind and be safe. He will be out of the way and we will all be able to get our work done."

After some reluctance, the other sisters agreed that this was a better plan. They would check on the baby at noon when they had lunch at home and if things looked dubious, someone would stay with the baby that afternoon. Then they left.

As Coyote rocked in the breeze, he debated whether he should nap while it was so quiet and comfortable or whether he should begin to free the salmon. He napped.

Noon came and the sisters found him sleeping peacefully. They liked their plan even better. During the afternoon, Coyote napped again.

For several days, that is all Coyote did. He relaxed and enjoyed the attention of his five mothers.

Finally, he had had enough of morsels and was ready for a big meal of fish. For five days, he slipped out of his cradle and went behind the lodge to make antler picks. He made a single pick each day. For the next five days, he made stone bowls. Each day he took a boulder and carefully cracked off a flat side and hollowed it out.

During this time, the youngest sister changed the baby's diaper and said, "Sisters, come look. Do not these ripples over his body look suspiciously like muscles? How could a tiny baby develop muscles? All he does is rock, sleep, eat, and fill his diaper."

"It is because we are feeding him so well," replied the eldest. "We are putting meat on his bones. That is all."

"I do not think so, sister," said the youngest. "This boy bears watching. I still think his eyes are too clever by half and he is waiting to trick us."

Coyote tried to look innocent, but he knew that his moment had come. Tomorrow he must break through the weir and free the salmon. He would take them upriver and become a hero to the people. No longer would they despise him as a fool, a coward, and a trickster. He would earn his rightful place as a leader of men, and women, too.

Next morning, as soon as the sisters left the lodge, Coyote released himself and gathered up his picks and bowls. He went down to the water and began to pick apart the trap. He worked in a hurry and made too much noise.

The youngest sister left reluctantly that day. Her suspicions were high. Her eye twitched and that was a bad sign. She did not go very far from home because of this and heard the sounds of the pick almost as soon as Coyote started.

"Quick, sisters. Come quick. Our fishtrap is being destroyed," she screamed again and again as she rushed to the river.

Coyote had already used up two of his picks. When he saw the sister coming and the others following close behind, he put the first stone bowl on his head.

The youngest sister swung her digging stick and pounded Coyote over the head, but the bowl broke the stick and the youngest retreated, screaming, "Hit him. Hit him hard, sisters. It is Coyote. He has been tricking us all along. I told you so. Kill him before he steals our salmon. It is all we have."

Each sister, in turn, rushed up to Coyote and slammed her digging stick down onto his head. Each blow broke a stone bowl he wore as a helmet. As the oldest sister struck, the last bowl broke, but so too did the trap.

Coyote dove into the water, calling back, "I will see all of you lovelies later when you have need of a man. For now, though, I will take these fine fish upriver and show them how they will fill the waterways with their nourishment. You should not have kept them to yourselves. Now you will only have the memory of them unless you go through all the pain and labor of catching them in the future."

After swimming a ways upriver, Coyote went to the beach and lay in the sun, drying off. The salmon warmed in the shallow water. When he was dry, Coyote built a fire and said, "Come here, some fine, young, firm salmon. I am ready to eat." Immediately a salmon jumped onto the sand and died. Coyote cooked and ate it, carefully returning the bones to the water where the salmon reappeared.

Coyote, of course, delighted in his new power over life and death. He continued upriver.

At the first village, he walked into the center shouting, "My people, I have a wonderful new food. It is a kind of fish called salmon. I will share it with you if you will share one of your maidens with me. I will marry her for the night and, in the morning, I will be on my way."

The adults met in council. A woman said, "This is Coyote. Remember who we are dealing with. He cannot be trusted. How can we be sure that he will do as he says. I certainly do not want any of my daughters spending the night with that vagrant. He is vile and nasty on his best days."

"You are wise to be cautious, woman," responded an elder. "But if this salmon is truly as good as they say, we will be well served to play Coyote's game. I vote that we risk it. We must make sure to allow only a plain girl to share his bed."

To this they all agreed.

Coyote had a wife in the village and, in the morning, he proclaimed, "Since you were not very generous with me, I will not be generous with you. I leave smallish salmon in your river. You will have to catch many of them to make a meal or to store enough for winter. That will be your fate."

Then Coyote continued upriver. At Chelan, he was refused entry to the village and proclaimed, "Henceforth, for your unkindness, you will have a waterfall between your lake and the river. You will get salmon only at the bottom of the falls. You will have no fish run of your own. That is your fate."

At each village and tributary of the Columbia, Coyote watched how people treated him and left them salmon or none accordingly.

At Kettle Falls, a huge gathering area, there were many people, much visiting, and abundant good times. Coyote married a beautiful, hard-working girl and he was delighted. In the morning, he said, "This is a wonderful place. I was very happy here so I will leave huge salmon at the falls. I bless the people who are here now and will be in the future." Then Coyote went on with his adventures.

For many years, salmon remained in the places where Coyote put them. They never went everywhere the way salmon do now. This came about when Salmon contested with Wolves for the daughter of a Methow chief. Her name was Mourning Dove. Salmon married her, but the Wolves enlisted the aid of Rattlesnake, who shot a magic arrow into Salmon's head, killing him. As Salmon drifted downriver in a canoe, his wife ran along the shore, sobbing and crying. Suddenly, she became a mourning dove.

Salmon went to the ocean and revived with the help of Mouse, who kept smearing grease over the bones. Since then, salmon have lived in the ocean, returning upriver to spawn and die. Every spring when the salmon runs begin, mourning doves greet them along the banks of the many rivers, welcoming them home.[12]

ANTELOPE
▼▼▼▼▼▼▼

"Who is that so far away, sauntering along the grassy plains?" Deer said aloud. "I will go and find out."

Deer came down from the woodsy hills and crossed the plains along a ridge so he could see the person he was going to visit.

"It is Antelope. He is my friend and I will race with him. Hello, Antelope," Deer called. "Do you want to race?"

"Hello, Deer," said Antelope. "I have not seen you for some time and my eyes are happy. Let us sit and visit for a while. We could smoke a pipe. When we catch up on the news, then we will race. But this time we must bet so the race will be interesting."

"Fine with me," said Deer and he sat down beside his friend. They talked of many activities and many old friends. They smoked some of Deer's tobacco and then a pipeful of Antelope's. They rested and enjoyed each other's company.

"We are caught up on the news. Now we can race," said Deer. "What do you want to wager? I do not have fine clothes or valuables. It will have to be something that either of us can give up."

"That is true," responded Antelope. "I think we should wager something we will not miss much. I will wager my gall bladder. It is small and I will not miss it."

"That is good," agreed Deer. "I, too, will bet my gall bladder. Where shall we race?"

"Right here is fine with me," offered Antelope. "It is my home and I like to run on the grass."

"But it is not my home," countered Deer. "I run through the trees on the mountainsides. If you win this race, then we will have to go into the forest and run through the terrain that is my home."

"Agreed," said Antelope. "Let us go down to the edge of that stream and run out across the plains to that far rock spire. The first to turn around that rock and reach the stream bank again will be the winner."

"My, but that is a long way," said Deer. "I will have to call upon all of my power to complete that course. I will start to sing my song now. I will be too winded to do it later."

"Do as you wish," coaxed Antelope. "I have only to wish and my power is with me. Sing as long as you like. Let me know when you are ready."

As they walked to the stream, Deer sang under his breath. When they got to the stream, neither took a drink, hoping that thirst would serve as an offering to put the powers on his side.

After a quiet moment, each alone with his thoughts, Deer said, "I am ready."

They stood together and tensed muscles. Deer sprang ahead first, but Antelope soon caught up and passed him, going far ahead to the rocky spire and heading back to the bank. Deer stayed behind.

At the end, Deer took out his gall bladder and gave it to Antelope, who put it inside. Since then deer have had no gall bladders.

After a short rest, Deer said, "Now it is my turn to win. We will race in the hills where my power works best. What will you bet?"

"I will bet my dew claws, these hard pieces on my heels. I never seem to need them," replied Antelope.

"That is fine," said Deer.

Antelope walked beside Deer until they were well into the forest on a rugged hillside.

"How will I ever run on this slope?" wondered Antelope. "These trees are so close together that I will not get through them."

"There is plenty of room," said Deer. "I run over this terrain all the time and I pass between trees with ease."

"Oh, well, that is your gift, but not mine," commented Antelope. "Let's race."

"How shall we go?" asked Deer. "Do we go around the hill or do we go over the hill? You choose."

"I want to go over the hill," responded Antelope. "Going around the hill would keep me lopsided the whole time. Going over the hill will at least give me a chance at winning."

"That is what we will do, then," agreed Deer. "We will start in that canyon and go uphill to the crest. From the top, we will go down a canyon on the other side and stop at the bottom."

"Fair enough," said Antelope. "I will probably be following you, anyway."

And so they ran, with Deer far ahead, up the steep hillside and down the other.

Antelope sunk to his knees at the bottom, while Deer waited nearby.

"You have won, Deer, and I could not keep up," panted Antelope. "Here are my dew claws from behind each of my hooves. They are yours now."

"Thank you," said Deer. "Everyone will admire my new feet and only hunters will know that I have no gall bladder when they cut up my body for food. So it will be from now on."[13]

SPIDER
▼▼▼▼▼▼

"Those ducks look good enough to eat," thought Spider as he came over a hill and looked down at a pond. "How can I trick them?"

He went into the woods and gathered together lots of twigs and branches and stuffed them into a loose bag he carried. Then he ran down the hill, wiping sweat from his brow. As he raced by the pond, a duck stepped beside him, saying, "Where are you going in such a hurry. Is something the matter? Is there an emergency we need to know about? What is going on?"

"I am hurrying with my bag of songs to a big gathering," replied Spider. "Many of them are new and everyone is anxious to hear them."

"Oh, in that case, stop here awhile. We want to hear them, too," called the duck. "Come here everyone. Come hear the songs that Spider has. This will be a treat."

The ducks came on shore and stood around. Spider said, "Form a ring around me. You must dance to appreciate my songs. You must shut your eyes very tightly. Do not look or the song will be spoiled."

"We will do what we have to," answered the ducks. They closed their eyes and danced. Spider began to sing, thumping on the ground with a stick to keep time. In his other hand, he waved a club and used it on the most plump of the ducks. He grabbed the bodies and pulled them into the center. He sang for some time before one of the ducks got suspicious of the irregular rhythms and peeked.

"Run. Run for your lives!" she called. "Spider is killing us." And the ducks flew off.

Spider regretted their loss, but there were many dead ducks to eat, anyway. He built a fire and buried the ducks in the ground to roast. He left their legs sticking up so he could find them again. Then he said, "I will take a nice nap after all of my efforts. When I awake, my food will be cooked."

He was just resting comfortably and was about to enter a deep

sleep when he heard, "Eeeee yeeee. Eeee yeee." He sat bolt upright
and looked toward the sound. He decided, "Two enemies must be
fighting to the death. Only they could make that kind of noise. They
must stop or I will never get any sleep."

Spider went toward the sound and found two branches of a tree
locked together. When the wind blew, they scraped against each
other and made a noise like screaming.

Spider said, "You must stop this at once. You live together and
you must not fight. I will pull you apart." He reached between the
branches and pried them apart with his hands, then he stuck his
foot between them. "Now you will go your own ways," he said. "I
will go mine." But when he went to leave, he was stuck. "Let go of
me this instant," he screamed. He pulled and he tugged. He
moaned, "You must let me go or my ducks will burn." But they did
not. Spider was trapped.

In time, Wolf came by and Spider called to him, "Help. Help
me. I have been captured by these branches and they are holding
me. You must free me or my food will burn. It is roasting in that
fire over there."

"Why should I help one so ugly?" said Wolf. "Your body is
bulbous, your arms and legs are skinny, and your hands are large.
I cannot even find words to describe your head. You seem fine right
where you are. Good-bye."

Wolf went away reflecting on Spider's words. "Did he say there
was food cooking nearby, something about a fire? Maybe he told
the truth. Maybe I will be able to eat my fill."

Sure enough, Wolf came toward a fire with lots of duck legs
sticking up. He sat down and wiggled a leg. "My, but this leg is
loose. These birds must be done to perfection. If I am very careful,
I will be able to get each one out whole and eat all of the meat off
of it." With great care, that is just what Wolf did. He ate his fill,
and then some. Then he replaced all of the legs into the fire and he
left.

Meanwhile, Spider waited in the tree. Eventually, the wind
picked up and blew harder. The branches began to bend and Spider
pulled himself out, saying, "Do whatever you want to. I no longer
care about your fate. Kill each other if you want. I am going away.
I will have my meal and depart this region. I leave you on your own.
Good riddance."

Spider climbed down and went to his fire. The smell of roast
duck filled the air. As he approached, his mouth began to water.

Soon he was drooling. He had been away many hours, and he was very hungry. He reached for the first leg, saying, "My, but these birds are well-done. The meat falls apart. I will have to dig each one out carefully so that nothing will be lost. First I will eat this leg, though." And he did.

When he went to dig out the body, he could not find it. "Could it be that all of the meat has cooked away? Will grease be all that is left of all those plump birds?" He dug deeper, and he dug faster. Nothing could be found, only the legs standing up.

He sat down to cry and moan. Then he thought, "Wolf did this to me. He left me between the attacking branches and he ate my food. I will hunt him down and kill him. I will eat him now that he has fattened himself on my meal." And Spider started off. He tracked Wolf. He closed in.

Wolf already suspected that Spider would take revenge if he lived. Wolf had a plan. He stopped and found a tree of soft, white wood. He took his knife and he made shavings. He put them in a pouch. Then he went on.

At a comfortable spot near the trail, Wolf lay down, scattered the shavings over himself, and became still. Then he waited. Soon Spider found him.

"Wolf, you are despicable," Spider charged. "You ate my food. Now I will kill you. Get up and fight." Wolf did nothing. Spider kicked him. Wolf did nothing.

Then Spider jumped back, saying, "My friend is dead. He is covered with maggots. He does not stink yet, but he is dead. I cannot eat him. He might be poisoned. I will leave. He certainly is foul."

And Spider went on his way, off to adventures of lust and stupidity.

Wolf got up, rubbed his stomach, said, "Thank you, Spider," and also went on his way.[14]

LOON
▼▼▼▼▼▼

"Mother," Loon woman asked, "where is my youngest brother? I have not seen him since the day he was born. You never mourned for him, so he must be living somewhere. Can you tell me?"

"Oh, you always ask me that question," the mother replied. "The one I named Floats Above has been lost for some time now. I am sure he is safe. Do not worry and do not ask anymore."

"She is lying to me. I know it," Loon thought. "When I find him, I will kill him. She must know that. She just wants to protect him. I am the oldest in this family. I have nine brothers and sisters. The younger ones get all the attention. If I start killing them, then I will become an only child. I will have everything I want. I will get all of the love around here."

The mother and daughter separated and went about their tasks. The day continued. At night, everyone came home, ate, and went to sleep.

Before dawn the next morning, as she always did, the mother went down to the spring to get water. This was her only time to be with her youngest.

Loon awoke and, driven by her jealousy, decided to follow her mother all of that day. "Mother will lead me to my brother," she thought. She went down to the spring.

"Someone has been swimming here," Loon woman said aloud. "The water is still swirling from the motion. Let me look for signs." After carefully looking around the edge of the pool, she found a long hair. "This is my clue. I will measure it against the hair of all of my brothers and sisters. Then I will know who is swimming here."

She went home. Everyone was awake and huddled around the fire. Her mother was cooking a quick meal.

"Let me look in your hair for bugs and dirt," Loon woman announced. "You want to start the day fresh and clean. I am the oldest and I will help you."

Her brothers and sisters were afraid of her. They sat there in a circle while she stood over each one and picked through their hair. In her hand, unknown to each, she held the long hair. She measured it for length and matched it for color. None of the eight had hair like that one strand.

She left the house, wondering who came to the spring. "I will hide at the spring until someone comes. I will wait and watch. Then I will know for sure."

She went back home. As she came in, she called, "Mother, I am going camping for a few days. I need to be alone. I need to meditate by myself. I am going to the high country. Fix me a small lunch. I will take it along."

Her mother was worried, but she did as her daughter wanted. Then Loon woman went to the spring. She hid in the brush nearby and she waited. She slept there at night, but was awake before dawn. No one came. She rested through the day and slept the next night. No one came the next day, either. This continued for several more days.

Suddenly, one morning, before first light, a handsome boy came to bathe. She could just see his outline and glints of his face and body in moonlight. Loon woman fell in love. She watched his every move. She suspected who he was, but he left before the dawn.

Excited, Loon woman went back home. "Mother, I have been away only a short time. Now I want to go back for a longer stay. Can you give me more food this time? I will be gone some time. Do any of my brothers or sisters want to come along? Do you?"

Her siblings held back, uncertain what she intended. Then the next oldest, a boy, said, "I will go along."

"No, not you," replied Loon woman. "Then I will go," said the next younger sister. "No, not you, either," snapped Loon. Six more times her siblings replied in the order of their birth and she refused each one of them. They now suspected the worst.

Loon went outside the house, and everyone followed her. Loon woman put her hand on the side of the building and called, "This one here, that is the one I will take along." Her mother gasped. All eyes were riveted to that spot. After a long pause, Floats Above came out and said, "You have found me out. I will go with you. A younger brother should respect his oldest sister."

"Come with me," replied Loon. "We will leave right now." And they did. They walked all day. At night, Loon called, "Let us camp here. It has been a very long day. We need to rest now. I will make a bed for us. I brought robes and pelts. It will be nice and dry. Just wait."

Floats Above stood to the side. He suspected that his sister was intending to commit incest, but he was powerful. He wished, "Make her fall asleep as soon as she lies down."

"Come, brother," Loon said. "The bed is made and it is soft. See, I can stretch out in comfort." Even as she did so, she yawned and fell immediately to sleep.

Floats Above put a log into his sister's arms and then he ran away. He rushed back to his home. When he got there, he screamed, "Get ready quickly. We must flee. I can only fool our sister for a short time. Then she will come for us and we will be killed. Run for your lives. Get ready now, I will protect us."

Floats Above went to the door and said, "Do not tell Loon which way or where we went." He went to the posts and the roof, to the mats and the spoons, to the cases and the packs. "Do not tell Loon where we are," he instructed each and every one of them. He thought that he had blocked all knowledge of their flight, but he missed one thing.

At dawn the next day, Loon woman awoke, hugging the log. She began to speak to her husband, saying, "I loved you from the first I saw you. I knew that you had to be around. I knew that you would be worth the wait. Now you are mine forever." Then her eyes focused and her hands felt the bark. She threw down the log, screaming, "If I cannot have you, no one will. I will kill you for this. I will kill you and all of your kind. This is too much. I have suffered long enough."

Furious, Loon rushed back home. No one was there. There were no footprints. There were no signs. Her family had vanished. Frustrated, she went to the door and kicked it, shouting, "Tell me where they went. Tell me immediately." The door was silent. She kicked each of the posts and demanded that they tell her. They were silent. She kicked the mats, spoons, bowls, cases, packs, and clothing left behind. None of them said a thing. She demanded an answer of the roof. It did not reply.

Livid with rage, she kicked the fire. "Why do you not tell me where they are. I can hurt you worse than they can. You better think about that. Someone tell me."

The ashes spoke up. Floats Above had ignored them. The ashes said, "Your family has gone to the sky. A basket came down for them and they went up, but they have not arrived to safety yet."

Loon ran outside and looked up. Her family was halfway to the sky. She began to sob and cry, "Come back. Come back. I will not hurt you. Why did you leave me? I belong to this family, too."

"Remember what I told you," Floats Above urged. "Do not look down. Do not encourage her. No matter how she sounds, do not pay any attention to her."

Everyone tried to keep looking up, but soon the mother looked down. The basket began to drop. Quicker and quicker it fell down.

Loon woman saw it. "Thanks for coming back," she called. "I will make a big fire to warm you. I will make you glad you came back. Hurry down. I will build up the fire." She rushed to get a smoldering ember from the fire at home and added limbs and logs to it. Soon a huge bonfire was raging in the clearing.

The basket shattered when it hit the ground and everyone tumbled out. Floats Above, however, rose back into the air. The other members of the family were dazed or unconscious. Loon woman threw them into the fire and added more logs. "There. All of you burn up now. This ends it. You are all dead. You left me and you should expect no better. I have had my revenge. It has been too long in coming."

Floats Above drifted away until he was over the edge of the Pacific Ocean. He floated down to the beach. Two Seagull girls came to him. "Who are you?," they asked. "We can hardly tell. You are so filthy and beat up, you could be anyone. What happened to you?"

"Do not ask," he said. "Help me wash off. Find me clean and dry clothes. You will not be disappointed."

The girls flew home and got soap and clothes. They brought these back. As they approached, one said to the other, "Look at that man in the sea. Is that the same one? He is nice to look at and he seems kind. It seems we have found our husband."

When Floats Above was clean and dressed up, they took him home. They married him. They were happy.

After a year, each wife had a baby. One had a boy and the other had a girl. They grew up very quickly. After a few days, Floats Above made each of them a bow and arrows. "Learn to use these," he said. "You will have need of them. They will be put to good use in time."

After a few weeks, Floats Above told his children, "There is a woman over that range of hills. She is Loon. She is mean. She killed our family. You must go and spy on her. Watch her secretly. Do not let her know that you are there."

The boy and girl went to the home of Loon woman. When they

saw her come out, she was mumbling, "Kill them. Kill them all. It has to be done. They deserve it." The children were so terrified by the very sound and sight of her that they ran all the way home.

They arrived panting and wide-eyed. "Do not be afraid of her," their father said. "I will protect you. She needs to die for what she did. You must help me do the deed. Go back and watch what she does. Only if we know her movements can we take her by surprise."

The boy and girl agreed and went back. They watched for a day. They went home.

The next morning, Floats Above got his family up and said, "Today we will have our revenge. We must go and kill that woman."

They got ready, filling their packs with sharp knives and arrows. They walked over the hills. The three archers surrounded the house. "Come out, hag," shouted Floats Above. "Time for revenge has come. My family has come to kill you for killing the others."

Loon came out and stood quietly in front of the house. "You cannot harm me. I am special. I am protected. I am safe. Do what you want. It will not hurt."

The father and children shot at Loon. They filled her body with arrows. She only laughed. She seemed unscathed.

"Well, brother, now you know," she chuckled. "Nothing can harm me. I can kill you anytime that I want to. You need to fear me. I do not worry about you. Do your worst, it will not hurt."

"Father, who is this witch?" the boy asked. "Why does she call you brother? Who is she?"

"I had hoped to save you from knowing this. She is indeed your aunt. But she is no kin to us. She killed your grandmother and all of your other aunts and uncles. She deserves to die."

"How horrible!" the children exclaimed. "We cannot be related to her. She must go. We will ask for help."

Loon woman stood and glared at them. She held her place.

The young girl spoke up, "Who will help us? This woman here has led a life that is not worth living. She has done us a great wrong. She must die."

No one responded.

The boy then called, "Who will help? This woman killed our family. She does not regret it. She must die."

Nothing answered.

Their father shouted, "This woman was never my sister. She abused my family and she tried to misuse me. She was not a good person. She needs to die. I wish it and so does every living member of my family. We only ask for help to do the deed. It has to be, so the future will know what is good and right."

It was quiet. Then Meadowlark flew close by. She whispered into the ear of Floats Above, "Her heart is in her left little finger. She will only be killed if you strike her there."

Now he knew. He took careful aim. Loon woman saw what he did and where he looked. Aghast, she threw up her hands to protect herself. It was a fateful move. Her fingers were exposed. The arrow struck her little finger and she fell down dead.

Floats Above told his children, "Now she is dead. She will do no more harm. The loon that is still in her will go to live in remote places. It will wear her necklace of white beads scattered over its shoulders. It will make a startling cry."

And so it came to be.[15]

BEAR
▼▼▼▼▼▼▼

"I hear that there are many berries ripe in the hills," said the young noblewoman to her women companions. "Let's go tomorrow and pick as many as we can. We will clean them and store them in boxes filled with fish oil. Next winter we will feast everyone on them and make our household proud. Now go to sleep and be ready to leave at dawn."

The other women who accompanied this high-class girl did as they were instructed. Only the slave women stayed up late getting big and little baskets ready and packing salmon to eat at midday.

At the first sign of light, the noblewoman was up and hurrying everyone else. In a gleeful bunch, they left the town in canoes paddled by the slaves.

The girl ordered, "We will go around that point of land and then up the second creek on the left. My family has always taken berries in that patch. It is ours according to the legend of our ancestor whose name is now carried by my second oldest brother. He was a great man with much power. He met and married a supernatural Martin near the place where we are going and that is how it got to be ours."

The other women remained quiet, letting the girl talk, as was her privilege. She was showing her worth and that of her family. For one so young, she was well-versed in the hereditary knowledge that make families high class. To know the history of her house and clan, along with those of the places where they went to get a variety of foods, was cause for admiration.

"She is truly high-class," the women whispered among themselves. Soon, a paddling song was started up to fill the time while they traveled. It was also a privilege of her family to sing this particular song. The slave women kept time to its tune.

"Here. Beach the canoe here," the girl called. "This is the end of the trail that leads to a fine berry patch. We will land here and go up the trail. My nephews have hunted here recently so that I know that the trail will be clear. They only warned us to watch for bears as they had seen spoor when they were here."

"Bears are such nasty things," replied her cousin. "They poop anywhere they want to. You have to watch where you walk, even on the trails. If only they would be more tidy, I would feel better about them. They are such majestic animals. They eat much the same foods as us, like salmon and berries. They sometimes walk upright. They howl and cry. When they are killed and skinned, their bodies look very much like ours. If only they could learn to be more tidy."

"Indeed," agreed another woman. "Still and all, however, we are all different and we must respect the ways of others."

The women went up the trail chatting and laughing along the way. The noblewoman moved to the head of the group and looked up ahead to gauge the distance to the berry patch.

"It is just up ahead," she called. "Just a little ways. Think of all those berries just waiting for us. Try to put more in the baskets than you eat. Come . . . Oh no, I have stepped in something."

Unaware, the high-class woman had indeed stepped into a pile of bear droppings.

"Those dirty things," she screamed. "They will leave their foul refuse anywhere. They are stupid, nasty things. They have no sense. They know no better. They are disgusting."

"Here, lady, come to the stream and we will wash off this foulness," crooned a slave woman. "There will be no damage, only this brief unpleasantness."

"Bears are despicable," continued the girl. "They mess up everything. They should learn better. They are animals!"

After a rest to clean up the moccasin and restore calm, the women continued on to the patch. Soon, they were happily picking berries, eating some and putting lots into baskets.

At noon, they had a leisurely lunch and then resumed picking. All of their baskets were full by the end of the day. There were so many baskets that everyone had to carry them, even the high-class young woman. This made her miffed because women of her rank rarely did labor, but it was shameful to waste what nature provided. The heavy baskets were carried on the back, supported by a padded tumpline stretching across the forehead. The young woman carried the smallest basket, supported by a tumpline and braced by her arms folded under the coiled bottom.

The women started back down the trail.

"I will walk in the back to avoid further adventures with bear dung," said the noblewoman. She was sullen as they started off.

They had gone only a short way when their leader cried out, "Oh, help me. My strap has broken and berries have tumbled out of my basket."

The women turned around and helped pick up the berries, bind the tumpline, and begin again.

They went a short ways and, again, the noblewoman cried out, "Not again. My basket has come undone and berries have spilled."

With less enthusiasm, the other women turned back and helped again. Then they went on.

A short while later, the same thing happened. All the women had to put down their own baskets and turn back to help. They were even more reluctant this time.

Again they went on. Again, the woman cried out, "My basket has come undone and berries have spilled." The women did not turn back. They went on, pretending not to hear.

Frustrated, the high-class woman sat down, stunned. She was surrounded by spilled berries. She did not weep because that was low class. She sat, knowing that eventually the others would return to help her.

From behind her, she heard a footfall on the trail and turned to see the shadow of someone coming. She was momentarily confused until a handsome young man came up to her.

"I heard your cry and have come to help you," he said.

Impressed by his manners and youth, the woman stood up and righted her basket. Together, they picked up the berries.

Then they set off, the woman following the man. She totally forgot about the other women and followed the man into the woods. After they had gone a considerable distance, the man reached up his hand to part a filmy gauze from in front of them. It was like webbing hanging among the trees.

Beyond, they walked on a clear trail that led to a bustling town. The man led the way to his majestic plank house, with a huge painted design along the front. The woman could not make out the full motif but she noticed ears, round eyes, and claws. Then her mind clouded over.

Inside the house, the man introduced the woman as his wife and his parents only nodded. Then the man went to his mother's brother, the master of the house, and introduced the woman. The uncle said, "Welcome, we have expected you for some time. We expect you to be dutiful as a high-class wife. You will manage the affairs of your part of the house."

The woman nodded, unable or unwilling to speak. She was as one mesmerized. She went to the cubicle of the house where her husband lived and began to inventory everything to know better her needs and duties.

A flicker of shadow startled her and she froze. Suddenly, she heard a voice. She looked in the direction of the sound. There, between painted and carved boxes, was a mouse, who said, "Princess, you do not know where you are or what has happened to you. You are living among the Bears. They were deeply insulted by what you said about them on the trail. They have brought you here for revenge. If you wish to live, you must do as I say. I will only advise you if you give me some of the grease you use as a cosmetic. Will you do so?"

"Noble mouse woman, I will do exactly what you say. My mind has returned and I am frightened. I will give you all of my facial grease and some of this mountain goat wool that I use as a puff."

"That will be fine," said Mouse and she accepted the gifts. Then she explained, "In a short time, you must say that you need to go to relieve yourself. You will go down to the beach, around the bend, where the women go. You will squat, but you must only pretend. Instead, take a bracelet from your wrist and break it up. Put the pieces under you before you stand up. When the Bears inspect the place, they must see only pieces of copper."

The woman did as she was told. She went to the beach and came back, knowing that she was being carefully watched and followed.

Shortly afterward her husband came to her and said, "We thought that you were like us and took great offense at your insults, but now that we see that you eliminate pure copper, we can understand how you were offended. We will be pleased to have you stay with us forever. We will truly be married."

The couple lived happily with the Bears for several years. Two children were born who looked and acted human. When the children were toddlers, the husband returned home to find his wife sad. He asked what bothered her. She said, "I miss my human family and I want to take the children to meet their grandparents and clan mates. They need to learn the history of their house and ancestry." The husband agreed.

The next day, he walked his family to the gauzy curtain that separated the Bear and human worlds and he held back the folds. The woman and children walked through and started into the forest. The wife glanced back for a final look and, there, where her husband had stood, she saw a bear dropping to his four feet and shambling away.

The family went until landmarks seemed familiar, then the woman knew her way. As she approached the town, she called ahead so that her kinspeople would not become frightened.

Rushing from the house, her uncle cried, "My daughter, we thought that you were killed. Your companions went back to get you and found bear tracks where you had been. We thought the worst. But now you have returned, and we know you are safe. Stay with us."

"Thank you for your concern," replied the noblewoman. "These are my children. They belong to our clan. Their father is the Bear whose tracks you saw near the berry patch. I have married and I will live there, but I want my children to know their relations and their place in the world. We have come back to visit."

"Oh, my dear," sighed the housemaster, "you have truly married well. We will enjoy your stay and we will send you back with many gifts for our in-laws. We will hold a feast in your honor and have many of our crests displayed so that your children can know their history and learn their pedigree." And this was done.

After several weeks, the mother said, "It is time for us to go home. My children now know about their royal house and I am pleased. Now we will go back to the Bears. In a year, we will come again to visit. That will be how we will keep in touch."

And so it happened. After the woman and children went back

beyond the gauze, they saw the Bears as humans. In a year, they came back to the town, only this time, the woman had started to grow fur. Her relatives were more nervous during her stay.

She and her family went home and came back the next year. Then she had bigger teeth and claws.

By the fourth year, she was quite like a bear, but her children continued to be human.

At the end of a stay when her relatives became increasingly uncomfortable, her uncle took her aside and said, "My dear, you are always welcome here, but you make us afraid. We are not used to Bears and regard them as dangerous. It would be best if you stayed with the Bears from now on. When your children are grown, we will welcome them back if they want to come and live with us."

. The woman and children went back to live with the Bears, where the noble lady died old and respected. Of her children, the son stayed with the Bears, but her daughter came back and married a human. She founded the Copper Bear House among their nation and left many descendants.[16]

TURKEY
▼▼▼▼▼▼▼

"Misery is all I ever know," thought the poor orphan girl. She lived in a pueblo long ago with only the turkeys she tended for company. Her parents and all of her close relatives were dead, killed by sorcery. She lived in the household of a woman of her Spruce Tree clan. This woman had many children of her own and, while she was not mean, she could not give much special attention to the girl. Instead, the girl talked to her friends, the turkeys.

"We think much of our girl," all of the turkeys agreed, but they kept their abilities to themselves. No one was to know how truly wise turkeys were. The birds lived in stone-lined pens located along one side of a smaller plaza of the village. There the girl came to them morning and night with grain and left-over food.

"The parrots who live in this town stay in rooms with the people.

How come we have to live out here in the open?" the turkeys often grumbled to themselves. No one had an answer, except to mention that parrots were much more pretty than turkeys, who were gray and drab.

While the pens were roofed with poles and adobe, the wind and rain got through. Fortunately, it was arid and so it did not rain much. Only during the winter did the turkeys have much to complain about. Then times were hard.

During a blizzard one winter, a chick who hatched late in the season was blown off the wall and broke his leg. When the girl came to the pens, she found the chick huddled in a corner, unable to stand. She picked him up and, fearing a scolding, took him home.

"Clan mother, a turkey chick has been hurt and I want to nurse it. Can we keep it here in our apartment?" asked the girl.

The mother, a kindly woman, replied, "It will not be safe. Many people come and go through our rooms. Your brothers and sisters will play hard with it and it will die. I warn you this will happen, but I leave the choice up to you."

"I will protect it," pleaded the girl. "I will tuck it away in a warm corner and only let the other children look at it. Only I will touch it. I will take very good care of it."

"It is your decision," replied the mother. "Do not be disappointed when it dies. It is frail."

"It will not die. I will tend it most carefully," replied the girl with confidence.

In the pens, the other turkeys were sure their offspring had died and that the girl had carried it off to save their feelings. Life went on as before. The girl fed the turkeys morning and night. During the day she nursed the chick back to health while his leg mended with splints.

"You are my best friend," the girl often told the chick. "No one else has time for me, but you do. I will take good care of you and you will grow old with me."

"This girl is truly lonely," thought the turkey. "I will not disappoint her. All of my relatives depend on her for food and shelter. She is very kind and does not make demands on me. I will stay with her."

Things continued in this way for some time.

One day, the priests of the tribe sent an announcer to each home who said, "We are about to reach the end of a long cycle of fifty-two years. The world may end. The times are very dangerous. Life hangs in the balance. Time itself is precarious. In four days we will gather in the plaza to dance and sing in a new cycle. All must attend. All must be of a good mind."

Every family and clan heard the news with dread.

The mother of the Spruce clan called her family together and explained, "We have reached a critical moment in time. The end of a cycle might or might not mean the start of another. It is up to the world to decide and we must help her. We must sing and dance and pray that she will choose to go on."

"Woe is me," moaned the girl. "I have only rags to wear. I have no men to weave a cotton manta dress for me. I am poor and I look it. I will hide in shame during the dance. No one will want to be seen with me."

The young turkey heard her and his heart filled with compassion. Before he could restrain himself, he said, "Do not feel sad. I will help you. All of the turkeys will help you. You are our friend and guardian. We will do all we can for you."

"You can talk," the amazed girl whispered. "Did you actually talk, or am I fooling myself? After years of taking care of turkeys, I know you are smart, but I am not sure how smart you really are."

The turkey tried to remain silent, but he could not. "I did indeed talk," he said softly. "Do not fear for your sanity. You did not invent language. I said it, and I mean it. Turkeys will take care of you. Just let me go back to the pens so we can talk it over."

It was evening and the girl had to feed the turkeys in the pen, so she took the grown chick along, under her arm. As she approached the pens, the other turkeys stared in wonder. Those in front called, "Look here, the little hurt chick has been healed. The girl is bringing him back. She is truly kind."

"Hello, everyone," called the young turkey. "Did you think me dead? I am very much alive. The girl nursed me and my leg back to health. I have lived in the houses like a parrot. It is noisy and crowded there. Believe it or not, we are better off in these pens because we have more time to ourselves."

"That cannot be," replied an old gobbler. "They are warm in there and well fed. Still, if it is loud and crowded, I would not like it. Maybe you are right. We will have a council and discuss this."

"Before you do, however," the young turkey interrupted, "we need to help this girl. You know the world might end in four days and all must attend the dance to become of one mind with the earth. This girl will stay away because she does not have nice clothes and jewelry to wear. We must give her some so that she can take part. We truly need her good wishes."

"Indeed, we do," all the turkeys agreed. After a brief meeting, a very old gobbler was selected to gift the girl with the needed articles. He came forward toward the girl.

"What do you want, old man?" the girl asked. "I know turkeys can speak. You can tell me."

After a quiet flurry of uncertainty, the older turkeys announced, "It was not wise for this girl to find out that we can talk, but we can and must trust her. Some of us will speak."

"Girl," they said, "you have been kind to us and we will help you. Your family is all dead because they were such good people. Sorcerers want the world to end in a few days so they will have ruins and corpses to use for their evil purposes. You will turn the tide and help the world survive. Even now sorcerers are meeting to cause a great flood to destroy the world. You must prevent it."

"I will do what I can," replied the girl. "I clearly remember my relatives as kind and considerate people. You must be right. They were killed so the world would end. I will avenge their deaths and renew the world at the same time."

"We will help you," agreed the turkeys. "Come back to us when everyone has gathered in the plaza for the dance."

During the next two days, the girl routinely fed the turkeys, but nothing out of the ordinary happened.

On the morning of the dance, everyone was excited and busy. Fancy clothes were cleaned and put on. Turquoise, shell, and colorful stones were worn as jewelry. Quietly and sadly, the girl left the house to feed the turkeys. While she was gone everyone gathered in the main plaza, well away from the turkey pens.

After she fed the turkeys, she stood still and waited. "Will you help me?" she pleaded. With those words, the oldest gobbler came forward and said, "Girl, stand in the corner and prepare to dress." The female turkeys formed a screen in front of her and one said, "Take off that old dress and hold it in front of you." The girl did so.

While the other male turkeys stood on the other side of the pens with their backs turned, the old gobbler began to make choking sounds. Soon, from out of his waddle (loose skin hanging from his chin), he coughed up a beautiful cotton dress, a painted wooden head tablet, and much fine jewelry of shell, turquoise, and precious metals.

"This is too good for me to wear," cried the girl. "I cannot go from poor to rich this quickly. What will people think? They will be sure I stole this."

"Fear not, daughter," the old gobbler explained. "People will not have time to think. They will know only that you are as pretty as you have always seemed. No one will question you, unless it be sorcerers. But they are now in hiding, awaiting their flood. Go to the dance and enjoy yourself. You must save the world. We have done all that we can."

Reluctantly, the girl walked around a row of houses and came into the main plaza with some trepidation. No one recognized her, not even her clan mother. All they knew was that a pretty girl had come to help and they were grateful.

They danced, sang, and prayed. The girl's movements were perfect and all admired her. She encouraged their good thoughts to work in unison and by so doing, she caught the attention of the world, who was pleased with their efforts.

Things were going well, when, from far off, people began to hear a dull roaring. They grew to realize that it was the sound of a rampaging flood caused by the release of the waters which had been trapped inside the earth. Everyone was afraid, and most ran to the tops of the highest roofs.

"Look all around you," an old woman screamed. "We are surrounded by a continuous wall of water. We will all drown."

The girl stayed in the plaza and continued to dance. "This is how I will save the world," she prayed.

From their pens, the turkeys rushed into the plaza and joined the girl in dancing. "This is how we will save the world," they also prayed.

Still the flood came. "It comes relentlessly closer all the time," the old woman screamed from the highest roof. "Someone must save us. The hills are too far away. We will never reach them."

Meanwhile, the young turkey who had been healed flew to the roofs and waited. "I will save the village," he prayed. "I will keep back the flood."

But still it came closer. It reached the bottom of the outer walls, which were solid to defend the town from attackers. The flood rose as if to climb the walls. Everyone wailed and moaned, but the girl and turkeys continued to dance.

Closer and closer the flood came to the top of the walls. Soon it would spill over, wipe everyone from the roofs and drown them inside their very own town.

Just then, the young turkey stuck his tail over the side and spread out its feathers, forming a fan. The flood froze in place. It came no higher. It did not reach the roofs.

Instead, by surges, the flood receded. In a short time, the water went back into the ground, dragging along most of the sorcerers. Only a few were left, but they were enough to assure sadness in the future.

Where the turkey's tail feathers first touched the foaming flood, a white rim was created. With each surge downward, another ripple was added to the tail feathers. To this day, turkeys have wavy bands of mottled color on their feathers and this makes them pretty. They also have a white rim at the very end of their tails and this is proof of their help during the flood.

Because the girl stayed calm and danced with the turkeys, people gave her great honor. She became wealthy and married well to a man of good family who treated her with kindness. When she had children, moreover, in recognition of her feat, they became members of a Turkey clan, a new family created in respect for all the help given by the turkeys. And sometimes, since then, turkeys have even been allowed to live indoors.[17]

PART FOUR

AWAITING HUMANS

▼▼▼▼▼▼▼▼▼▼▼

More of an end product than a divinely planned original, humans take their place in the world only late in its creation. Like tiny mammals in the age of dinosaurs, humans were offstage and shadowy creatures until many other things got sorted out and the general order and outlines of existence were in place.

Twins are often the avatars of humans or their coming. As paired males they have each other for company and protection, but they need to find women to marry and set up homes. Often, the twins are themselves the product of a union between a divine father and a virgin human mother. Throughout the Southwest, the world was put in final order by twin Warriors who were born after the Sun came to earth and gave their mother two pinyon nuts. These twins started off visiting their father and gaining the power to slay various monsters. Later, their success went to their heads and they began to kill with abandon. Haunted and pursued, they were taught a lesson by one of their victims who was sent after them by the spirits. The incident in this story comes midway in their career when they befriend an old couple in a dysfunctional town.

The proper food for humans receives much attention during this time. Cannibalism becomes forbidden under most circumstances, and various animals are defined as noxious and inedible. Building on the theme of hoarded food, the Cherokee tell the story of Kanati and Selu. The version given here has been generalized to emphasized the contribution of man as hunter and of woman as farmer.

Throughout the East that was the pattern. Men provided the meat and women the grain. The labor that they had to expend to do so came about as a consequence of this story with another set of twins.

In the cold north, hypothermia and freezing presented their own threats. Cannibalism was always a danger in the struggle to survive. Athapaskans of the western subarctic had bogeymen called We-chuga, but the most famous of the monsters with a heart of ice were the Windigo, who threatened many a northern Algonkian community.

The showdown between humans and animals took many forms in stories across the continent. The most famous account was told by the Cheyenne. Among these hunting tribes, the hunting of food and of women was expressed in countless jokes. In this version of the Great Race, the wound of an arrow could have come as easily from the bow of Cupid. The buffalo cow changes from prey to wife and after many tests, the family lives happily ever after. Here as elsewhere, family meant the most open and caring collection of people, both humans and others, that lived and worked together.

The arrival of humans on the face of the earth was not sufficient to explain the differences among tribes. Where an ancestor came from the sky, cavern, sea foam, or prior being, people had to move and migrate to find their present homes. As one example, we learn the origins of the Hidatsa nation of the Upper Missouri River in modern North Dakota. With their nearby town and earthlodge-dwelling cousins, the Mandan, and their camp and tipi-living relatives, the Crow, out on the Plains, the Hidatsa represented a range of options for life on the northern grasslands. Rather than having a common origin for all, the three Hidatsa villages traced their ancestry to the earth or the sky.

Hidatsa origins become all the more momentous and poignant in the light of history. Lewis and Clark spent their first winter in 1804–1805 among the Mandan and Hidatsa north of modern Bismark. Several thousand people were still alive, having survived a smallpox epidemic in 1782. During the next few years, however, disease and devastation further reduced the population. Then, in 1837, smallpox came among them again. Several hundred people were reduced to a handful. Only about three dozen Mandans lived through it. Yet these few continued the elaborate rituals which several hundred had enacted for centuries. And these few labored mightily to remember all of the traditions that they could. It is a testimony of their resolve that their complex origins could be recorded in the 1930s and retold into the next century.

TWINS
▼▼▼▼▼▼

"Come, younger brother, we will travel. There are still many monsters in the world and our father the Sun has given us powers and weapons to overcome them."

"Brother, you always take the lead. What shall we do now?"

"We will go to the village of stingy people and we will teach them a lesson. First we go to that beehive near the spring three hills over from here. Let's go."

The twin brothers jogged over land to the spring, stopping there to drink.

"Now that we are refreshed," said the elder, "we need to build a fire and smoke the hive. That will stun the bees for a time."

"Here are sticks," replied the younger. "I have my firemaking kit with my bow drill. I will ignite an ember by rotating the shaft of my fire starter." He squatted down and used the looped bowstring to twist the shaft while he sawed back and forth with his bow. Soon, an ember glowed at the groove in the board holding fine wood shavings. He blew gently and the ember turned into a flame, which he used to burn a stick. Other sticks were added and soon a smokey fire was going.

The elder twin took some smokey sticks and held them under the beehive. Soon the bees were groggy.

"Now the bees will help us, brother," he said. "Grab some handfuls of honey and smear it all over your body."

"Unh, this is sticky. Are we going to present ourselves as sweet morsels to the girls of that village?" the younger one asked.

"Be serious. We must look like poor orphans so that we can test these people. When your body is covered, do as I do. Roll on the ground and make the dirt stick. We must look like we have not bathed in years. Muss up your hair. Shred your loincloth. Make yourself look disgusting."

The younger twin did so. Soon they were filthy and pitiable. Then they went on.

At the edge of the town, they went from door to door. They did not knock or enter. They only stood there.

At each door, they heard, "Go away, you filthy boys. We do not feed orphans. We do not like the homeless. Go on your way. We do not want you here."

"But we are hungry. We will not mess up your homes. We will eat outside. Where is your hospitality? How can you send away the poor and hungry? That is not the proper way. You must have compassion."

"No, we do not. We take care only of our own. How do we know what diseases you carry or what nuisances you can be? Go away."

Slowly, going to each house in turn, the twins went through the village. Always and everywhere, they were rejected.

Just beyond the ring of the village there was a lone house. The twins went there.

At that door, they heard, "Come in. Make yourself at home. We, too, are poor. We have little food, but what we have we will share. We are only an old couple. We never had children. We are pleased you could visit us. Please stay as long as you like."

"Grandparents, we are indeed grateful," answered the twins. "You are the only kind people in this village. Why are you not respected and revered? Why doesn't everyone else follow your generosity? Why do you not have more say around here?"

"We are old and feeble," the old man replied. "That is why everyone treats us badly. We are descended from the founders of this village. Our ancestors lived here. Then young people came seeking refuge from enemy attacks and we let them stay. Soon, they took over the town and made us move out here to live separately. We do not hate them. They are young and foolish, but they will not learn. They will not behave properly. They are greedy and selfish. How could the world survive with such attitudes?"

The old woman added, "We hoped they would be like the children we never had. But they were not. They do not give us food or presents like elders get in other villages. We keep hoping they will learn to behave. I have a small garden and so we have corn and beans. Sometimes my husband kills rabbits and we have meat to flavor our gruel. Today, we have only cornmeal and that will be your food."

"Thank you, Grandmother," the twins murmured as she dished out the mush. "We are very hungry and are grateful for anything."

After tasting the food, they smiled and said, "You are a very good cook. This mush is tasty. It is truly good."

"I have cooked for many years," she replied. "I have learned a few tricks that others do not know. They are uniquely mine." The old man smiled when she said this, but he did not reply.

After eating, the twins asked, "Can we hunt for you? We can add to your food supply quickly."

"We would be most happy if you did so," the old man chuckled. "But if you hunt for us, you must stay some time with us. We do not want you to run off immediately. Having you around might teach everyone else good manners."

And so the twins settled in. Soon the house was full of meat. Meals were plentiful. The couple ate better than ever before, and everyone else noticed it. The couple ate better than anyone else in the village.

Behind their doors, people grumbled. "Who are those filthy boys that they hunt so well? They must be witches. We should run them off or kill them. That old couple do not deserve to be treated that way. They are soon to die and need to be ignored."

The twins pretended not to hear, but their ears were very keen. They heard these remarks and kept track of them. Revenge would come.

Late one night, the village met in council. A bully spoke up. "We must do something about that household. It is unnatural for boys to live with old people. They are not related and yet they help out. I do not understand it. They are friendly, outgoing, and helpful. Who needs this? We need a spy to find out what is really going on. Let us send a girl to entice them."

After much discussion, a girl was selected. She was a middle child who watched her older and younger siblings get all the attention, while she was barely tolerated by her family.

"I am only doing this," she said, "because I never get special treatment. No one likes me. If I find out what you want to know, then you must treat me better. I want special foods and mats. I want a fine necklace. Promise me these, and I will go. Otherwise, find someone else."

People were used to such greed, so they gave in to her. No one ever thought to honor the promises, but still they agreed in order to get their spy.

The next day, the girl followed the twins when they left the house. After some time, she caught up with them and started talking.

"You boys are certainly very nice to that old couple. Do you expect to inherit from them? You know that they never had children of their own? They have very little, so you will not get much. If you started a home of your own, you would do much better. But then you would need wives. Maybe you already are married back where you came from. You could still marry here, though. Big families are important. You can rely only on relatives to help you and feed you."

"She does blabber on," the older whispered to the younger. "What do you think she wants? A family of her own, or is she a spy?"

"Definitely a spy," nodded the younger. "We will have to be careful. We do not want to give offense just yet. We will have to humor her. We could always play that she is our wife?"

"Brother, do not jest about such things," scolded the older. "This village is already bad enough as it is. We do not need to add that to the mix."

"You spoil all my fun," mocked the younger. They kept on walking, listening to the girl go on and on.

As they were about to crest the top of a hill, the older brother said, "Quiet, everyone. We are about to hunt, and noise will scare away the animals."

"No one talks to me like that," the girl scolded. "If you are so rude, I am going home." And she did.

"Well, at least, we are free of her," responded the younger twin. "It is nice to have peace and quiet again. We will even be able to hunt. The animals will not be running from the sound of her voice."

"That is true," said the elder. "Let us split up. You go that way and I will go this way. Kill what you can and meet me back at the house."

After hunting for a few hours, both brothers killed deer and brought them back slung over their shoulder. They met as they got near the home of the old couple. The girl was there, waiting nearby.

"My, but you are both great hunters. I never saw a single deer the whole time I was walking in the country. You must have considerable power to have made them come to you. You will be valuable husbands, if you are not already."

The brothers feigned exhaustion as they each carried a deer and so could avoid talking with the girl. Still, she persisted.

"That old couple do not eat much. What will you do with all of the venison? Surely, you cannot eat it all yourselves. It will soon go bad. You had best give some of it away. My family will help you. Give me some to take home. We will have it for supper."

"We are happy to share," said the elder. "My brother and I will butcher and clean this deer and you can have the other to take to your family."

"But we only like the haunch," she said. "It will be too much work to clean the whole deer just for that piece. Why don't you clean both of them, and then I will take what I want."

"She certainly is demanding," the younger whispered. "I could never marry her. I would get no rest. I have had enough. These people have no manners. I am fed up with them."

"Maybe now is the time," the older whispered back. Aloud, he said, "My brother and I already have stored much food with the old couple. Here, you can have both deer. Take them to those in need. Share with them. Eat your fill."

Shocked, the girl stood there, and the older brother magically wished the deer to shrink to the size of dogs. Then he draped them over her shoulders.

"Now take them home," he ordered the girl. "We have had enough of you. Feed your people and learn good manners."

In a great huff, the girl carried off the deer. From afar, she called back, "I'll show you. You cannot insult me that way. I'll tell everyone that you tried to molest me. Then you will see who your friends really are. You will learn your own lesson."

When she got home and threw the deer down, they magically resumed their full size. Her family was impressed with all the meat, as were the neighbors.

"Where did all this meat come from? Did you seduce the boys? Did you steal it? You were only supposed to spy on them. This is going too far."

"Leave me alone," she sobbed. "Everyone is yelling at me, and all I am trying to do is to get some nice things and special food. Those boys are too nice most of the time."

"What will happen to these deer? Are they yours? Will you share them? After all, you were working for us when you got them."

"I have had it," the girl screamed. "Take these stupid deer and eat them all up. I never want to see them again. Go on. Take them."

And so everybody did. They roasted the two deer and ate their fill.

"I am stuffed," everyone agreed. "We all need to take a long nap." And so they did.

"This is what we have been waiting for," the older twin told the younger. "All defenses are down. We will have no opposition in body or in mind. Tell the old people to hide in the backmost storage room with the dry corncobs. Tell them to stay there."

The younger brother did this. "We will hide in the corn room," the old couple agreed. "We have given up on these people. Do with them what you will."

The twins sat in the middle of the plaza, singing softly. Sometimes, they alternated verses. Sometimes, they sang together. Their song released the souls of the villagers and they became canyon wrens living in the nearby rocks. Then, over the course of the night, the bodies and houses turned to stone, providing a reminder to everyone else of the dangers that come from not sharing and not helping out.

With the dawn, the brothers called the old couple to come out into the sun. As they emerged and stood outside, the old man looked at the old woman and the old woman looked at the old man and each exclaimed in unison, "You have become young again."

"Indeed you have," said the older brother. "You can now start over. You will now have children and you will raise them well. When they are grown, move down to the river bottom and build a fine town. Everyone will delight in visiting you. You will teach everyone else how to live properly and how to behave as decent people."

Before they left, the brothers washed off the filthy honey and their faces and bodies shone with health and strength.

"We always suspected you were not the vagrant orphans you pretended to be," the old man mused. "Still, whatever your origins and pedigree, we were pleased to have you with us for a time as our children."[18]

HUNT AND HARVEST
▼▼▼▼▼▼

"Son," his mother asked, "who were you playing with today? We heard your laughter from down near the stream. You sounded like you were having a good time."

"I do not know who he is," the boy responded. "He comes out of the water and calls me 'brother.' He says that his mother was cruel and threw him into the water."

Harvest, the mother, was stunned. She mused, "I know all of the local children. This strange boy is not one of them."

She looked at her husband, Hunt, who said, "Listen carefully. You know that I always bring back game whenever I go hunting. That is my gift. You also know that you take this meat down to the stream and butcher it. Then you wash off the blood in the stream. That boy is the blood returned. I warned you that something like this would happen. Blood is a sacred thing. It gives life. Now it has given life to this other boy."

Hunter turned to his son and said, "Tomorrow, when that other boy comes, offer to wrestle him. When you have your arms around him, hold him until I come." The boy agreed.

The next day, the boy went down early to the stream, eager to see his new friend. As he approached the bank, the other boy came out of the water onto the beach. "Let us wrestle," the son said. "I will beat you," said the other. After they had rolled on the ground for a time, the son had his arms around the chest of the other and called, "Father, come quick. I have him now."

Hunt and other men rushed down to the beach and grabbed the strange boy, who screamed, "Let me go! Let me go immediately! You threw me away and never gave me a care. You abandoned me."

"Quiet, boy," the father said. "We only mean to help you. You cannot live this wild way. You need a home and family. We will give these to you. Come along and behave."

At the house, Harvest asked, "What shall we call him, this new son of ours?"

"Wild will be his name. We will keep him indoors until he calms down." It took a long time, but Wild did come to his senses. Yet he was mischievous and often led his brother astray.

Wild learned the routines of his new home. He saw that whenever Hunt went into the hills, he came back with a deer or turkeys. He was never empty-handed.

Wild said to his brother one day, "Let us follow Father tomorrow to see how he hunts. He has great skill and we can benefit from observing him at close quarters." Reluctantly, the brother agreed.

The next morning, they shadowed Hunt as he went into a swamp. Wild turned himself into a fluffy feather and drifted onto the back of their father. He watched Hunt cut some reeds, add feathers, and straighten them. Then Wild willed the fluff to drift back to the shore. He changed back into a boy and said, "Our father has made arrows in the swamp."

Staying out of sight, the boys followed their father up a high hill. At the top, Hunt lifted a huge rock and a deer came out. He shot the deer and carried it back down the trail.

"Our father keeps all the deer confined in that hole," whispered Wild. "When he wants venison, he lifts the rock and kills a deer with his reed arrows. Now we know. That heavy deer will slow him down. If we hurry we can reach home before him."

The boys did so and were playing by the stream when their mother called them to supper. They had fresh venison.

A few days later, Wild coaxed his brother into going back to the cavern. "Here is what we will do. We will go into the swamp. I will make seven reed arrows, just in case I miss. Then we will go onto the hill, lift the rock, and shoot a deer. Everyone will be proud of us."

The brother was not so sure, but he went along anyway. At the peak, he got to lift the rock. As he held it up, Wild stood at the ready. Except that he was too slow. As soon as the rock was lifted, a deer emerged. A moment later, another deer came out. And another, and another, and another.

The boys were transfixed. They were confused. They were flustered. Finally, as a deer ran by, Wild reached out with his arrow and cut off its long tail. The boys liked that and began to chase after all the deer and bob their tails. Since then, deer have had short tails curved over their backs.

Meanwhile, the hole remained open. Other animals came out. These were raccoons, rabbits, muskrats, and many other four-footed creatures. Then came the birds such as turkeys, pigeons, grouse, and woodcocks. They darkened the sky and made a rushing noise.

Sitting at home, Hunt heard the sound and rushed outside, saying, "My sons have been bad. They have caused trouble. I will have to go and see how much of a disaster they have created."

Trudging up the hill, Hunt saw the boys frolicking with the animals. Furious, he said nothing. Instead, he went into the cavern and removed the lids of four pots. From each of these came either lice, gnats, fleas, or mosquitoes. These swarmed over the boys, who screamed in pain. They were bit and stung. They were in agony.

When they could not stand any more, Hunt brushed off all the insects. He made the boys stand while he lectured them. "What did you do? There was always food when and where you wanted it. You never had to work hard. I got enough food for everyone. I made things easy. No more. You have messed up all that. You have let out all of the game. From now on, everyone will have to hunt all day long. They will have to rely on luck and skill. Food will not be the sure thing that it was. You have done wrong. Go home to your mother. I will have to hunt for our meal and, even then, I may not get anything. That will be your fault."

Quietly, the boys went home. Everyone knew what they had done so they hid inside. "There is no meat," their mother complained. "I will have to get you something else."

She took a basket and went to the storehouse nearby. It was raised on posts, so she had to climb a ladder to get into the small door. After she was inside for a time, she came out with the basket full of beans and corn.

"How can all of those seeds come out of that tiny room?" Wild asked his brother. "Tomorrow, we will follow mother and find out how she does that."

"Oh, no. Not again," said the brother. "We have already done enough to mess up the world. Leave things alone. They are fine just the way they are."

"Fine," snapped Wild. "Be that way. I will go by myself. I will learn the secret and I will not tell you. You will never know. So there." The other boy relented.

The next evening, when Harvest had gone into the high room, the boys climbed up the back and removed some clay chinking from between the wall of poles. They saw Harvest standing in the center of an empty room with the basket on the floor in front of her. Leaning over, she rubbed her stomach and corn kernels cascaded into the container. She rubbed her armpits, and beans fell into the basket. When it was filled, she lifted it up and carried it down.

The boys jumped down and rushed home. They were waiting when she got there. She knew what they had done and was very sad. "Mother, your food is disgusting," shouted Wild. "I will never eat it again. It is filthy and unnatural." The other boy cried when he heard his brother speak, but he said nothing.

The mother sat down and spoke softly. "I must feed you something. You do not like what I can give you now, so I must make other plans. I will die. Do not try to stop me. It is for the best. After I am dead, but before my body grows cold, dig up the large field in front of this house. Take out all the grass and weeds. Then drag my body over that fresh ground. Make a spiral seven times. Bury my bones in the middle. Go and sit on the edge of the field. Stay up all night. Do not doze. Do not sleep. In the morning, I will feed you again."

She dropped down dead. While her son began to prepare the field, Wild tied a yoke around the body and got ready to drag it over the exposed earth. "Hurry up," he cried. "The body is getting cold. You must hurry."

"I can never do this whole field," the boy despaired. "Here, I have made seven patches. Drag the body over them." This was done, so now fields are small and scattered. The next morning, as promised, the corn was tall and ripe. Since then, however, people have not been able to stay awake all night and the crop has been slow to mature.

The same morning of the first grown corn, Hunt returned home. "Where is my wife?" he asked. "She died," people told him. "The boys made her ashamed and she died, so we now have to work hard in the fields in order to eat corn."

"That is the last straw," the husband sobbed. "I want nothing more to do with those monsters. They have ruined everything. I am going to live with the Wolves from now on." And he did.

Wild turned himself into a feather fluff again and settled on the back of Hunt's shirt. When Hunt got to the Wolf town, everyone was meeting in the council house. He walked down the long tunnel into the round chamber under the earthen roof piled up to look like a hill. The Wolf leader sat in the middle and said, "Please sit down, stranger, and state your business."

Hunt explained, "At home, I have two very bad boys. In seven days, I want you to go there and play stickball with them."

"We understand," said the Wolf. He knew that meant that in seven days they were to go and kill the boys. "We will do that," the Wolves agreed.

"Fly me up through the smokehole," Wild wished for himself. The fluffy feather went up and out of the rotunda. As it landed on the ground, Wild returned to his human shape. He ran home and warned his brother.

The next day, they began their preparations. Wild gave the orders, "Run back and forth around our house, except for the section that the Wolves will cross. Make four bundles of arrows and put one in each corner. When all is ready, we need to hide in the woods nearby."

On the seventh day, the boys were hiding when the house was totally surrounded by Wolves. As they moved closer, they passed beyond the trail made by the boys. Once inside, it turned into a huge fence that shut in all the Wolves. Moving among the stockpiles of arrows, the boys shot and killed most of the Wolves. Only a few escaped into the swamp, and many of these were killed when the boys set fire to the swamp. Only a very few Wolves survived.

Satisfied with their defense of themselves, the boys then decided to find their father. Wild said, "I will roll this hoop in each direction. If it returns, then our father is not there. When it does not come back, then we will know where to go to look for him." After many attempts, the hoop remained in the East.

"Our father is there. If we go there, we will find him," Wild told his brother. They went. After days and days, the boys came to Hunt, who was sitting with a small dog beside him.

Hunt greeted them by saying, "You have been very bad. Yet, you came to find me?"

"Yes, we did," the boys replied. "We always accomplish whatever we try to do. We succeed in all things. We have become good men. We sent a hoop to find you and it seems that it did. It is now that dog beside you."

"Four days ago, this dog came to me and it has become my friend. It seems that your thoughts toward me have been good. Since you have found me, we will go together. I will take the lead."

They wandered for some time. Once they came to a swamp and Hunt said, "A horrible monster lives there. It is best to avoid that place." And they went on. When their father was out of sight, Wild turned to his brother and remarked, "We better see what is in that swamp. It is best to know these things. The unknown often causes more trouble than the known."

Reluctantly, the brother followed Wild into the swamp. Creeping along they came to a giant panther asleep on a hillock. Standing on either side of it, the brothers took turns shooting arrows into each side of its head. The panther awoke and looked from side to side but was neither hurt nor upset by the wounds. Unfazed, the panther went back to sleep. The brothers moved on.

When they caught up with Hunt, he asked, "Did you find it?"

"Indeed, we did," the brothers responded, "but we could do nothing with it."

"You were lucky. Now you must be on your guard. We are coming to a village of Cookers. They are called that because they cook and eat people. They are cannibals. Beware. Do not do anything stupid. Try to be sensible. I will pass on. I will not visit the village. I know better. But that is not the case with you two."

"We will behave," the brothers said.

"I will see that Wild keeps us out of trouble," the son added.

"I can do that for myself," Wild said. "Look here. That is a tree struck by lightning. Let us gather up some of the splintered trunk and take it along."

As they approached the village, people rushed out, crying, "Welcome. Welcome all of you. We really like people. We like them husky and young just like you. We will have a grand feast with you. Come to the meeting house."

Once inside, the boys watched while the fire was built up and a huge pot of water was put on to boil. Outside, they heard everyone being called into the hall for a feast. Wild was grabbed and thrown into the pot before a lid was placed on top of it. His brother watched from the side, unafraid and unperturbed. He knew his brother's abilities. To help, the brother added kindling to the fire, secretly including splinters from the lightning-struck tree.

"The meat must be done by now," a leader announced. A cook went to lift the lid. As soon as he did, a blinding flash filled the house. Lightning ricocheted through the building, killing all of the cannibals. Then it left through the smokehole.

The brothers appeared outside the hall as though nothing unusual had happened. They hurried on to catch up with Hunt. When they did, all he asked was, "Did you survive?" "Indeed we did," was all that they had to say.

The family kept traveling. They came to the eastern edge of the world where the Sun comes out. Hunt disappeared and the brothers waited until the next morning to find their way. They climbed through the edge and walked up the dome of the sky. Soon they came to Hunt and Harvest sitting together.

"Welcome, children," they said. "Please visit with us for a time. Then you must move to the West. That is where you will live from now on."

"We are happy to do so," the sons exclaimed. "You seem happy and healthy. We are delighted to know this. We will stay for seven days. Then we will move to the West. That will be our home." And so it is to this very day.[19]

WINDIGO
▼▼▼▼▼▼

"Gather around, children. Move close to the fire. Get as warm as you can," urged the old woman. "I will explain what just happened. Do not be afraid. It is over. He is dead. Soon he will be burned up and his ice heart will melt. Then he can never return.

"That huge man that was just killed by our hunters was a Windigo. We did not know it for some time. He was like that for several years."

"How did he get that way?" a boy asked. "Was there something wrong with him or with his people? Was he always like that?"

"No," the old woman said, "he changed into a Windigo. Before that he was like you or me. He grew up and married. He had two children. He hunted well. His family and friends were well fed. People liked him."

"What happened?" a girl asked.

"We can never be sure. By the time that people get to be Windigo they have lost the ability to speak. They only live to kill and to eat other people. That man's wife and family died. That must have been when it happened. Despite all of the spirits who helped him and the game that he killed, a bad winter came a few years ago. Starvation stalked the camp. His wife boiled up bones and hides to make a soup. That helped for a time, but it was not enough. A blizzard came and they were snowed in. There was nowhere to go and no way to hunt. They had no food. The man began to ponder his fate and that of his family.

"If a man has any doubts or his spirits do not come to help, a man can begin to think the worst. Bad things happen. The man begins to chew on his own fingers, then he chews on his lips.

"The more hungry he gets, the more he chews. Soon, he has no lips and all hope is gone. From then on, he becomes a Windigo. This man killed his own wife and ate her. Then he ate his children, leaving the youngest and most tender for last.

"He lived through the starvation, but his family did not. His heart turned to ice and he became a Windigo, but he hid it from us. He said that he came back to the village to get help for his family, but when he returned, they were gone. They became lost in the blizzard and died of exposure. We believed him.

"Sometimes dogs and children would disappear, but life is hard and we thought that they had wandered away and died of exposure. Yet we never found any remains. A Windigo eats everything. He even crunches the bones into powder to eat. That is why there were no remains.

"This winter has been hard again. We are starving and the Windigo waited. A boy went to check his traps, hoping to bring back food. The man followed him and the boy died. Other hunters coming back to the village found the Windigo feasting on the warm, bloody flesh. They were tempted, but they had good help.

"They attacked the Windigo with spears and clubs. They forced him to his knees. Then they cut off his head. Keeping the head and body apart, they built this huge fire with all the wood in the village. They burned the body and then placed the head into the flames. They fought hard to keep head and body separate.

"Now only the ice heart is left. When that burns and melts, the Windigo will never come back. They are powerful beings. They live only to eat. They live only to survive. They care for no one else. They can outlast anyone. They can live through the most bitter cold."

The woman paused in her account. She had been chewing on her lips. Blood trickled down her chin. Soon she too would be warm and well fed.[20]

BUFFALO
▼▼▼▼▼▼

"Why is that?" the man pondered. "I had a strange dream. I shot at a buffalo, but my arrow went beyond him and hit another one far away. I have had this same dream for four nights now. What does it mean?"

"It seems peculiar, but hardly something to worry about," the old man answered. "Ignore it and it will go away."

"But I cannot," the man replied. "The day is just starting. I will take my bow and arrows and I will hunt for bison. Then I will find out what it means."

The old man said no more, and the man went off to hunt. From a hill he saw a small herd wandering toward a stream. He hid in the nearby brush and waited. He took careful aim at a bull buffalo, but his arrow skipped away to strike a young cow. "Now my dream has come true," the man thought. "That must be what it meant."

While he watched, the cow turned around a few times with the arrow hanging loose from her side. She wandered away and the man followed. The cow kept just ahead of him. When she went around the side of a hill, the man went over the top to head her off, but he could not get to her. He followed her all day until sundown.

Then he gave up and went home. "Tomorrow I will follow her trail. She should be dead and I can get the fresh meat." He went to sleep. The next morning he found and followed the trail. It went across a long flat prairie. He walked for miles. Off in the distance, he saw a tipi. He went toward it. When he got close to it, a boy came out, saying, "Father, welcome. My mother is ready. Food is prepared for you to eat."

The little boy took the hand of the man and led him inside. "Welcome, husband," a young woman said. "Our child has been waiting for you to come. I have cooked wild turnips and berries for you."

The man ate. "Your food is very tasty," he said.

"Thank you. I wanted to make something you like. Tomorrow, we will move camp," she said.

That night, the man and woman slept together, like a married couple. The boy had his own bed.

Before dawn, the man awoke, staring up at the sky. There was no tipi. There was no family. "All I can see are seven stars shining in the sky. They are the brothers who help the dead find the way to the afterworld. But I am not yet dead. I had best look to the living."

He got up and searched for tracks. Eventually, he found marks going in the direction of the bison herd. By midday, he again saw the tipi off in the distance. He had found his family. The boy came out and led him in. The woman fed him. They went to bed. The next morning, they were gone.

The third and fourth days were the same, except that on the last day, instead of a plain, he climbed up a high ridge. Beyond it were buffalos filling all of the space that he could see. There were millions of bison.

As he followed the footprints through the herd, he came to a place where they turned into hoof marks. "The woman and boy have become a cow and calf," he said in wonder.

Indeed, the calf came to him, saying, "Father, you had better go back. They will try to kill you. First they will test you, but they expect you to fail. They will have many calves lined up and you will have to guess which one is me. I will help you by shaking my right ear. But do not guess me immediately. Wait a few moments. Then point me out. They must not know about our trick."

Soon a huge bull buffalo came to the man, saying, "You are not welcome here. You kill our kind and show little respect. You do not even know your own family. For that you will die. Stay where you are and I will prove it. All of the calves will gather and you must pick out your son."

"I know my own," was all that the man said.

"All of you little ones. Line up. Form a straight line. We must show this man a lesson," the old bull called out.

The calves lined up. He quietly walked up and down the line. He saw a right ear shake. He waited. He stood back. Then he pointed, "That is my son." And it was.

The herd grumbled. "Try him again. It was an accident. He cannot really tell one of us from another."

The calves scampered about. The son rushed by the man and whispered, "I will wiggle my tail."

The young bison lined up. The man watched closely. He walked the line. He saw the tail move. He waited. Then, again, he correctly found his son.

The herd was outraged. "That cannot be. It is just luck. He cannot do it again."

But the man did, with his son's help. And he did it a fourth time, too.

The herd was angry, but they could not hurt the man. He had proved his worth. Instead, the old bull called, "Everyone leave here. Go across the river. We need to be done with this man."

As the herd swam across the river, the calf came to his father and said, "Go over to the side of that hill and dig up the root you will find there. It will keep you from drowning in the river. It will keep you safe."

The man did so and, using the root, made it safely across the river. The herd bellowed and pawed the ground when they saw him cross safely. Some of the old buffaloes gathered together to plot revenge.

The calf came up to the man, saying, "Father, my grandfather is not happy with you. He will find a way to get to you. The test will continue. They now plan for you to race my grandfather along a narrow ledge. He will try to crush you against the side or pitch you over the edge. He will offer you the choice between a red stick and a black stick. Choose the one on the outside so he will not get the chance to crush you. Be very cautious and careful. Run fast and keep away from the edge. Do your best."

The old bull came up to the man. He said, "If you insist on staying around us, you must race me along that ridge over there. You can choose your position. Here is a red stick and a black one. Your choice will determine your location. We will know what it will be when you choose."

"I choose the red stick on the outside," the man responded.

"Then that will be where you run, along the outside of the ledge," the bull replied.

The father and the grandfather walked to the ledge. They eyed each other. The bull pawed the ground. They were ready. They started to run. Halfway down the ledge, the old bison and the man were side by side. The bull turned to gore the man and throw him over the edge. The man saw the movement and dropped to the ground. The buffalo bull could not stop. He went over the side and crashed below. He died.

Enraged, all of the other bison came together. They changed into human beings. They sat down. The elders formed an arc in the middle. They called the man to them. "Please shake our hands. You are brave and have done well. Now we will make a truce. Only one more thing is required. There must be a great race. Everyone will run. All of the buffalo and all of the other animals will run. It will be a marathon. We will call all of the creatures to come here." This they did.

All of the animals gathered. All of them were opposed to the man, except for Magpie and Crow. These birds chose to run on the side of the man.

Everyone took a long time painting and dressing up. Each animal put on the colors and the decorations that it still wears today. The Bald Eagle put white clay on its scalp. The Antelope smeared yellow all over his body and added white splotches. The Skunk painted on black and white stripes.

As they dressed up, the animals talked about wagers. "If I lose, I will howl and live in the hills," said Coyote. "I will fly high into the sky and live on cliffs," remarked Eagle. "I will live among flowers and be silent," added Butterfly. "I will live in the dark, wet ground," called Worm. In this way, all creatures found their callings and abilities.

Finally, everyone was ready. They started. The fastest animals forged ahead. The man was close to them, but not in front. They ran for many hours and many miles. Over them all, Magpie flew higher and faster than anyone else. It was Magpie that won the race. That meant that the man had also won.

Everyone stopped and gathered. The eldest buffalo called the man to him, saying, "Well, you have won. Everything from now on must be done according to the wagers that were made. Every species and life form will have its own ways. Our meat, our skins, and our bones will be yours for the taking."

"Thank you," the man said. "I never meant any harm. I will show respect and care for all of you. I will love all of my relatives. We will all be related. I know that if one of you had won, humans would now be your food. We must depend on each other from this day forth."

"In addition," the elder said, "all of us will give you help. We will teach you the Sun Dance and give you parts of ourselves to extend the power of the ritual."

There, in the Black Hills, a special lodge was built and the animals taught the man the correct ritual. The course of the Great Race goes around these hills. It helps to make them sacred forever.[21]

HIDATSA
▼▼▼▼▼▼

EARTH ORIGINS

"Who are you?" asked Lone Man. "I have been wandering all over, but I saw no one else. I thought I was the only being in the world."

"I am First Creator," the other responded. "I, too, thought I was alone. Where are you from?"

Lone Man said, "I come from the west, where the grass is high. My father was the grasshopper called Stone Buffalo. I never knew my mother."

First Creator said, "I had no mother. I had no father. I come from the water."

"Now that we have met," said Lone Man, "we must decide who is older. Then we can begin to make the earth."

"Fine," agreed First Creator. "We will have a contest. Whoever is older will be able to survive anything. I will plant my staff here and I will die. You decide how you want to test longevity."

"I am not sure," said Lone Man. "I will wander the earth to decide." And he did.

Many years later, Lone Man wandered by a few tiny shreds that remained of First Creator. The staff still stood nearby and Lone Man plucked it up, convinced that he had outlasted the other. At that instant, however, First Creator jumped up and declared, "This proves that I myself am the older and the more hardy. I am senior to you and I will decide about the earth."

"What will you do?" asked Lone Man.

"I will request help from the birds to bring up mud from the bottom of the sea. I will approach Goose, Mallard, Teal, or Mudhen to dive."

In turn, Goose failed. Mallard failed. And Teal failed. All of these birds failed. With little hope, Mudhen was asked to dive to the bottom. Mudhen succeeded.

"This bird has dived to the bottom of the sea and brought up mud for us," said Lone Man to First Creator. "We can now make the earth."

"Take half of this mud," First Creator said to Lone Man. "You make land on that side and I will make land on this one. We will let the sea run between them. It will become the Missouri River."

They set to work. First Creator commanded, "This will become land east of the River. It will be filled with plants over a huge flat plain."

Lone Man made the western lands. "It will be filled with bison and animals," he said. "It will have mountains and rugged steppes."

The men met again and agreed to inspect each other's work. Lone Man said, "The east is too flat. Things will not stay there. It must have something done to rough it up."

First Creator stamped his foot in frustration and it left a dent.

"That is just the thing," remarked Lone Man. "We will scuff up the land with our heels. That will make it uneven and able to hold things."

Laughing and jumping, that is what they did. They scuffed up the eastern lands.

First Creator looked over the west and said, "There are too many animals. Some of these should be sent away. Those spotted cattle and maggots do not need to be here. Let us send them away to Europe." And this was done, but later the maggots came back as Europeans.

Now the world was ready for other people. First Creator said, "Let us summon people from the underworld. I will make a hole and have a vine grow through it. People will climb up that."

Many people climbed up this sturdy vine until a pregnant woman started up. She was too heavy and the vine broke. Since then, people have lived above and below the surface of the earth.

First Creator said to the people, "Scatter over the earth. Divide up into small bands and speak different languages." And people did.

Of particular note among all these tribes and bands were the Mirokats at Devil's Lake. These were the ancestors of several groups who became the modern Crow and Hidatsa. At some distance lived the Mandan, close relatives who gave many traditions to these other tribes.

At the village at Devil's Lake lived two brothers, Hungry Wolf and High Bird. Hungry Wolf was married, but High Bird was not. One day, the wife of Hungry Wolf offered water to High Bird, who refused as a good brother-in-law should. To have accepted the drink would have been a signal to begin intimacies.

The wife was hurt by the rebuff and, to her husband, accused High Bird of accosting her. Hungry Wolf plotted revenge against his brother. He believed his wife without reason.

He went through the village announcing that he was gathering a war party. Men joined him and began to dance. High Bird also came to his banner. The men went down to the banks of the river and set off in many bull boats. After they had paddled for several days, they camped on a small island.

That night, Hungry Wolf went to the other members of the party and said, "My brother has tried to compromise my wife. He should be punished. Tomorrow before dawn gather at the boats and push off. We will leave him here to starve."

When High Bird awoke, he was alone, stranded on the island. His companions were long gone. He wandered the island, but found no food or shelter. After many hours, he fasted and prayed. The Sun came to him and said, "My son, I know you are innocent. You have been wronged. I will help you. Here are four balls of mush. Take them to the shore and summon aid. A large serpent will rise from the water and carry you to land. Feed him one of these balls at intervals so that the last ball is given to him on the other shore. From now on, I will come to you whenever you need help."

The man went to the shore and called, "Grandfather, take me across the water. I have mush balls to feed you."

From the depths of the water a huge head arose and said, "Grandson, I will do as you ask. You must watch the sky, however, for any signs of a cloud. That will be the Thunderbirds, my enemies. If you see them, then we must turn back."

High Bird nodded and got on. At intervals, he fed an offering to the snake. Off at the horizon, a whiff of cloud appeared, but High Bird would not mention this because he wanted to get home. As they reached land, High Bird gave the last ball to the snake, pausing long enough for the cloud to hover overhead and strike the snake dead with a lightning bolt.

A handsome man appeared beside High Bird and said, "Thank you for your help. That serpent did much wrong and only helped you because he was forced. You have done us all a kindness by helping me to slay him. I will aid you when needed." With that the Thunderbird disappeared.

High Bird wandered over the plains. It took him days to get his bearings from the night sky. In time, he saw a weeping man. He watched from a distance, wanting to stay in hiding for his own safety. Finally, the intensity of the man's grief drew him out. He went closer.

"Why are you crying?" High Bird asked. The man turned and High Bird discovered that it was his orphan friend who had been mourning his supposed death. "Do not weep," High Bird cried. "See, I am alive." The friends embraced.

"Everyone thought you dead," the orphan sobbed. "Come home with me now and we will show them the truth."

When they got near the village, High Bird found a mourners' camp had been set up by his relations who thought he was dead. "Mourn no more," High Bird shouted. "I am alive. I have returned."

Stunned, his mother came to him. "My son," she said, "I never thought to see you again. What happened to you? Were you betrayed or wronged?"

High Bird took his mother aside and explained the misunderstanding with Hungry Wolf.

"But this is very wrong," the mother said. "I need to make it right between my sons. What shall I do?"

"Mother, you must go to my brother and ask for enough tobacco for one pipeful. When Hungry Wolf gives that to us, then the breach will be ended," explained High Bird.

The mother went immediately to Hungry Wolf and asked for tobacco. He refused her, his own mother. She went back to High Bird, and he sent her again, and again, and again. Four times she went and, four times, she was refused.

The relatives despaired. "What else can we do?" they asked each other. Eventually, it was decided to send mourners with seven singers to the home of Hungry Wolf to sing tobacco songs every day for four days. Still he refused. Now, the mourners prepared for the worst. They dug very deep holes with coverings because they knew that revenge would come from the sky.

The Sun appeared to High Bird and said, "Things are very bad. Brothers should never fight, especially over their wives. Soon I will eat human flesh."

High Bird stood in the center of the mourners' camp and shouted, "Take cover. Hide yourselves deeply."

Then came a "whoosh" from on high, and a celestial fire scorched the earth. The mourners were saved in their deep cellars, but all others were killed, except for the wife who started it all. From that time on, she has been named Calf Woman and used as a warning that married women can cause trouble among people.

From the survivors, the Hidatsa, Crow, and Awaxawi separated and went their own ways. People lived by hunting, but they started to show less and less respect for life.

Once, some foolish Hidatsa hunters killed a buffalo cow and teased its calf. They cut it and kicked it and treated it shamefully. The spirits were outraged. Since the Awaxawi were not involved, they were warned to seek a high place. They moved to Square Buttes along the Missouri River.

Water rushed out of the ground and rain fell from the sky, flooding the world. Only a few people were saved, along with the Awaxawi. When the water receded and the land dried, these people wandered away. In time, they met the Awatixa and both eventually joined with the Hidatsa, who had learned about the proper ritual and physical care of corn from the Mandan. Each tribe maintained a separate village along the Knife River of North Dakota. The Crow moved on, far into Montana, taking with them the tobacco rites.

As a reminder of the flood, the scuff marks of Lone Man and First Creator became lakes throughout the east.

SACRED ARROWS

"What is that sound? It seems to be bellowing," Charred Body said to himself in the sky. He went over to a fresh hole and exclaimed, "Look, down there is an unknown world."

Charred Body lived in the sky in one of four earth lodge villages there, each a day apart from the others. Charred Body took the form of an arrow and sped to earth. He saw that the sound was coming from the throats of huge bison living in herds. After he landed, the spirits who already lived there decided to destroy him. They sent one of the most powerful of the monster spirits to do this, but Fire Around Ankles only managed to singe the feathers of the arrow.

Charred Body decided to populate the earth. Magically, he built thirteen earthlodges. Each was made by excavating the earth into a circular depression, setting up four sturdy corner timbers to support the roof, and covering the whole framework with stringers and crosspieces holding up layers of grass, matting, and dirt. When finished, the lodge looked like a domed hill of earth. These substantial dwellings protected people from the bitter winters of the northern plains.

When the houses and village were done, Charred Body went

back to the sky and selected thirteen young couples. "Come with me to the land below and found a new society," he said to them. "I have houses all ready for each of you to live in and fill with your children to come. In time, each of these thirteen lodges will become one of the thirteen clans living in different villages."

The couples changed themselves into arrows and followed Charred Body to the earth. When the village was well established, First Creator visited Charred Body and was invited to smoke with the men. First Creator expressed his concern, "Everyone in this village is happily married and will look to the future, except for Charred Body, your leader. I will take him to another village where he can marry the daughter of the chief. We will go now."

First Creator and Charred Body went to this village, where they were well received. Food was put before them as they sat at the honored place at the back of the lodge. Soon the girl was brought in to meet Charred Body. Her father said, "Daughter, this is an important man who has come here to meet you. You should be honored."

But the girl responded, "How can that be? I have never heard of him. He must be some foreigner with filthy customs. He cannot be worth my time." Insulted and enraged, Charred Body killed her, and fled.

The chief mourned his daughter and plotted revenge, saying, "Monster spirits, I summon you to attack Charred Body and his village. Destroy them utterly for what they have done to my beloved daughter. Let no one survive." First Creator had remained behind to mediate the situation, but he gave up the effort when he learned these plans, knowing that such a heartfelt summons would unleash devastation on the world.

First Creator summoned Meadowlark to him and said, "Go to Charred Body and warn him to protect himself and his people." Meadowlark did this, but the monsters made Charred Body forget the message. Knowing there was no defense, Weasel lured Charred Body away from the village, and First Creator hid his sister in a remote corn crib. Then the monsters destroyed the village.

After the destruction, Charred Body came home to the ruins. He grieved for a time, but then he built the first sweat lodge to revive his determination and to keep himself healthy. He said, "Hereafter, people will use the sweat lodge to tend their wounds and sorrows. It will make people feel better."

Charred Body's sister was found and taken to the new lodge.

Two men were assigned to hunt for her because she was now pregnant, a promise of renewal for the village. Every day, she stayed at the house, cleaning and cooking. Charred Body had told her, "You must remain alone until the birth. You are now our only hope. Do not receive any guests. Do not provide welcome to anyone."

Still, the monsters plotted total annihilation of the community. Headless, a powerful monster, came to visit, looking like a distinguished old man. "Surely, such a fine old man can do me no harm," the sister thought. She welcomed him. "I will cook you a roast," she said. "While it bakes we can have a long visit." She put the meat on to cook, and conversed with the old man. She was delighted with his company.

When the roast was done, the old man said, "Daughter, it is a mark of my respect for the animal whose life was given so that we may eat that I only take meat from a platter held in front of me. Taking food from a pot or a plate on the ground seems a cold thing to do."

"Very well, Grandfather," she said, "I will serve you. I now put the meat on this platter and I will carry it to you. I will hold it in front of you while you cut off what you want."

As she stood before him, her huge belly protruding over the platter, Headless lashed out with his long fingernails and ripped open her stomach. She collapsed and died. From the gaping wound, Headless took out a fetus and threw it into the eaves of the house where it became Lodge Boy. A second fetus began to wiggle from the womb and he threw that into a nearby spring. To compound the tragedy, Headless propped up the body of the mother and twisted her mouth into a grin. Then he left, saying, "This serves them right. A woman has died for a woman."

When Charred Body returned home, he saw his sister's smiling face and greeted her warmly. She did not welcome him. She did not respond at all. Brothers and sisters stayed away from each other as adults, but Charred Body went close to her out of concern. "Sister, are you ill? Can I help you?" Then he saw the blood. He was horrified. He keened and mourned greatly. After a time, he took his sister outside and gave her a scaffold burial.

From the shadows of the lodge, Lodge Boy watched all of this. He stayed hidden. The two men returned from hunting and learned of the murder. They sat down in the lodge, distraught. From the corner of their eyes, they saw a flicker of movement. Then they saw the boy. As one sat blocking the view, the other crept up and captured him.

They said to Charred Body, "Look, here is a baby. All is not lost. A life has been saved from all this destruction. We will raise him as our own. They calmed Lodge Boy, cleaned and clothed him. They hunted for him and fed him. He grew into a man.

One day, the hunters returned to find a buffalo tongue with teeth marks on it. "Who did this?" they asked Lodge Boy. "Every day, another boy comes and plays with me," he said. "I do not know who he is but he seems like my brother."

The next day, the hunters pretended to go away. When Spring Boy came into the lodge, they blocked the doorway and captured him. They tamed him. While they were cleaning him, Spring Boy spit out many shells. Then he grew up strong. He was always more adventurous and daring. When he found the grave of his mother, he revived her. When he heard about the monsters threatening the world, he and his brother went out to the four directions and killed them.

Charred Body warned the twins to take their arrows with them and stick them in the ground when they slept at night. The arrows would warn of danger if they fell over. Several times, they were thus alerted to the approach of monsters and were able to kill them.

Finally, even the spirits of the sky world became worried about all these killings. Long Arm, a sky leader, came down to punish Spring Boy and took him to an arbor in the sky for a slow death by torture. Since Spring Boy had done most of the killing, the spirits were most keen to avenge themselves on him.

When Lodge Boy awoke, he found his brother missing and went all over the earth as a flying arrow. He could not find Spring Boy. Sadly, he returned to their camp and pined. He looked up and saw the hole in the sky through which Long Arm had taken his captive. Lodge Boy went through the hole in the sky. After walking only a short way, he came to the home of an old woman who befriended him. She told about the coming torture of Spring Boy. Lodge Boy went with her to visit the place, but then left quickly when the spirits started to become nervous.

That night, Lodge Boy came back and freed Spring Boy. On their way out, they captured Long Arm's stone ax despite its having ever-watchful eyes. This was a great coup. Moments later, Long Arm awoke, missed his ax, and ran to the hole. He covered the hole with his hands, but Spring Boy said, "Take your hands away unless you want to lose them. I will chop them off with your own ax."

Long Arm responded, "You have won my ax, but I will let you free only if you promise to observe below the rites that you witnessed here in the sky. They will warn people to do things in moderation. Destruction can be carried too far, but so can good deeds."

The twins returned to earth and took new names in honor of their deeds. Lodge Boy became Big Medicine and Spring Boy became Black Medicine. Assuming the shape of arrows, they traveled all over visiting people and spirits.

While they were walking over the prairie, they came to a huge wall. "What is this thing? It blocks our way. It is solid, yet it breathes." The brothers walked in opposite directions along it and discovered that it was a very long snake with two heads.

"We cannot go around it because of the mouths at each end. It is too high to fly over. What will we do?" Big Medicine asked.

"We can burn a hole through it," answered Black Medicine. He made a fire and applied it to the side of the snake. When the hole was big enough, they climbed through, but on the way, Black Medicine's hand touched the side of the passage. A bit of cooked flesh came off and rested in his hand. "This smells good, like cooked meat." And he ate it before his brother could warn him.

Within minutes, Black Medicine was writhing on the ground. "Oh. It hurts so bad. My insides burn and my head hurts. Brother, please help me. I cannot stand this."

Big Medicine looked on as his twin began turning into a snake identical to the one they had just killed. "Brother, what can I do? It is too late to stop the process. You are doomed. What can we do?"

"I am of the water," Black Medicine said. "Carry me to the Missouri River so I can become one of the seven Grandfathers in charge of the river. I will live there. Come to visit me to bid me farewell with all my relations. Make offerings of seven cornmeal balls. I will respond to offerings and prayers for long life and for safe crossing in bull boats. People will make these by sewing together buffalo robes over a domed willow frame. They will enable people to travel over the water."

Big Medicine was now alone. He asked his brother what he should do and was told, "We need to have a child to carry on our work. Powers such as ours need to pass from father to son."

So, the twins decided to have a child. They found a virgin and asked her to bear a child. Then they wished her pregnant, saying, "When he is born you must give the boy the name of Unknown

Man." Just as the woman gave birth, she died. The baby was raised by his mother's mother and mother's brother. As he matured, the twins transmitted their power to their son, which also enabled him to become an arrow.

The boy grew into a man and a good hunter. He killed so many animals that he needed help to carry and butcher them. The daughter of a lame Gambler in the village came to his aid as a way of getting meat for her family. In time, they married. Because the old Gambler was lame, his family stayed near him in the village when everyone else went on the winter hunt.

The twins came to visit the new couple and, as a kindness to their new in-laws, they said, "We will doctor the Gambler." As one of them sang and smoked, the other removed snakes from his legs. When the snakes were sent away, the Gambler was healed. In this way, Unknown Man and his wife learned curing rites and passed these on to future generations.

"We must feast my fathers," said Unknown Man. "They have been good to us." So the twins and everyone else were feasted. When the twins left, they promised, "We will send a herd of buffalo to your village to express our own thanks in return."

Bellowing and snorting, the herd arrived the next day. The animals fell dead just outside the village and special women ritually butchered them. Because of their conduct, Unknown Man proclaimed, "These women will establish a special order called the Holy Women. It will take in members who are prominent women skilled in domestic tasks." And this was done.

Soon, scouts returned from the winter hunt to take back food stored at the village. They had been unsuccessful. Very little meat had been taken. Aghast, thinking that starvation threatened, they arrived at the village and exclaimed, "Where did all of this meat drying on the corn scaffolds come from? There were no herds like this on the plains. We must hurry back to tell everyone to come home. This is where the meat is." Expecting starvation, the villagers returned home to plenty. Unknown Man and his family were much honored.

One day, Unknown Man followed a lone bison onto the plains. Every time he took aim and fired, the arrow was magically deflected. With flinty resolve, Unknown Man followed after the buffalo until it led him into a hollow hill where a man, a snake, and a buffalo lived.

Standing in front of them, the man said, "Unknown Man, you will lose your memory and become my servant. You will do all that

I say. You will be unable to question or to respond." And it was so. For a long time, Unknown Man did all that he was told, without will or memory.

Finally, one day he looked into a spring and saw his own reflection. "I know who that is," he shouted, "but I cannot recall his name." As he tried and tried to recall, Unknown Man regained the memory of himself. He was weak from the long period of neglect, so he called for aid. "Fathers, I need your help right now. Only you are strong enough to save me. I have been captured and my will stolen. It has returned, but I have no strength or ability."

The twins came and killed the snake and the man. The buffalo implored them, "Spare me for I, too, was a captive. If I am spared, I will teach you to make offerings to assure that there will always be buffalo. You must give sage sprigs and speckled eagle feathers to bison skulls at household shrines or whenever you find one out on prairies. That will show respect for my people and we will be grateful and never leave."

And this was done.[22]

▼▼▼▼▼▼▼

As a reminder that stories continue to live now as always, two brief versions are given here.

SNAKE

"I am going fishing," the man said. He left the yard and went down to the stream. He began to dig for worms and forgot about everything else until, out of the corner of his eye, he saw movement in the grass and looked down. There was a snake with a frog in his mouth.

"Hello, Mr. Snake," the man coaxed. "Have you brought me a present? You know how much fish like frogs to eat. I will be sure to get a big catch. Thank you."

He took the frog, but the snake just stayed there.

"Oh, sorry," the man apologized. "I should give you a gift in return. That is the Indian way. All I have is the drink in this flask. I brought it along to keep me warm. Here, have a swig."

And the snake did. Then it left.

The man went back to digging. As he was kneeling down to gather some fresh worms, he felt something poking on his leg. He looked down.

"Hello, again, Mr. Snake," he smiled. "Have you brought me another frog? You are very kind." The man took the frog and put it in the can with the other frog and the worms. Then he took the flask from his back pocket and gave another swig to the snake.

"Thanks again. I have enough bait for fishing now," the man said. The snake left, and the man went to the bank of the stream and sat down to fish. He baited his hook and leaned back. Soon, he felt poking on his leg and looked down, saying, "Mr. Snake, you are too kind. You give me more than I need. Let this be the last of your frogs. Here, take a big belt from the flask."

And the snake did. It left the frog with the fisherman and went straight as an arrow through the grass. It had had so much to drink that it could no longer slither.

FALLING ROCKS

"Times are hard," the old woman complained. "It has not rained in many years and meat is in short supply. We must send out a scouting party to find us a new home."

"Agreed," assented everyone in council.

Four scouts were asked to volunteer and four men came forward. These were Big Thunder, Sky Seeker, Falling Rocks, and Swift Current.

Standing before them, the old woman said, "Each of you must head in a different direction to look for a place where there is food and water. When you have found it then return to us. If you are away for more than a month, either come back or send word so that we know that you are well. You must keep us informed of your progress."

"We will do that, Grandmother," the scouts replied in unison. Then they went on their ways.

The village tried to survive until their return. They fasted and prayed. They made offerings. Each searched his or her consciousness for omissions and guilt. They sought to restore harmony and balance to the world.

Swift Current was the first to return, saying, "I found a small valley to the west where there is a spring. Many creatures come there to drink. There will be water and food. Many seed plants grow there that will also feed us."

The people were happy, but they decided to wait some more until other scouts returned.

After a month, Big Thunder sent word back that he had not found a suitable home. He was managing to get by, but there was not enough to supply the whole village. After another few weeks, he himself returned and said that things in the north were bleak.

Sky Seeker had sent back meager word, but he indicated that there was hope for a new home in the south. After two months, he returned and said, "There are large herds where I just came from and big lakes filled with water. We should go there."

A council was called and the decision was much debated. Finally, all agreed to go south. The old woman ended the discussion by reminding them that no word had been received from Falling Rocks. "We have not heard from him. When we move, we must leave a message for him so he will know where to find us. He went to the East, but that is all we know."

So a big signboard was left at the place where the village had been, telling stragglers that they had gone to the lakes in the south.

For many years, people waited for word from the missing scout. Eventually, other people came from Europe, which was to the east. Villagers asked, "Have you seen our missing scout or do you know what happened to him?" The Europeans did not know, but, as an expression of the concern they shared with the native people, they also put out signs along their roads to remind everyone to "Watch out for Falling Rocks."[23]

APPENDIX: SCHOLARSHIP
▼▼▼▼▼

A host of scholars, some of them Native Americans as well, have contributed to our understanding of traditional American literatures. Even before there were professionals, interested laymen put together collections of stories.

Stephen Powers, a journalist, traveled through much of Native California in the 1870s and collected many tales and useful information about surviving Native peoples. Later he did the same in Ireland.

Among the earliest professionals, active during the latter half of the 1880s, was Daniel Brinton, a Philadelphia physician who edited a series called the Library of Aboriginal American Literature, which popularized classics such as the Popul Vuh of the Quiché Maya and, more dubiously, the Walam Olum attributed to the Delawares but probably produced from foreign sources.

Relying on Native folklore collectors like Henry Tate and William Beynon for the Tsimshian, and George Hunt for the Kwakiutl (Kwakwaka'wakw), Franz Boas amassed a great store of myths and stories. Around the turn of this century, mythology became a focus for Boasian research because it was distinctive of different cultural backgrounds, readily acquired both in linguistic transcription and English translation, and a strongly empirical means for tracing the historical movements of traits and motifs from tribe to tribe and region to region (Waterman 1914).

Boas (1935) felt that culture was "reflected" in mythology both as detailed ethnographic information encapsulated within the content of stories and as secondary explanations, provided by the tales themselves, which integrated traits from disparate historical sources into the coherent patterns of a culture.

In his classic account of Tsimshian mythology, Boas (1916) was able to draw from the texts valid ethnographic information on house construction and occupation, social structure, kinship, prestige system, rituals, religion, supernaturals, and cosmology, while at the same time suggesting an interior origin for the Tsimshian, which more recent research has discounted. Most recently, the careful ethnopoetic translations of stories by John Dunn (1988) has revitalized Tsimshian research, which has also benefited from the recent publication of Marius Barbeau and William Beynon archival materials (MacDonald and Cove 1987).

Paul Radin treated Native mythologies as literature in its own right. In "Literary Aspects of North American Mythology," Radin (1915) explicitly rejected an earlier theory that every text had a primary version by showing that plots, episodes, motifs, and characters could and did shift from one version to another of the same narrative or of different ones. Although Radin's primary work was among the Winnebago (1923), he also studied Californian and other Great Lakes tribes.

In the mid-twentieth century, Melville Jacobs, a Boas student, used a body of linguistic texts he had previously collected to probe into the psychological dimensions of literature. Using stories and, most particularly, mythic characters, he drew inferences about the anxiety-provoking conflicts inherent in Clackamas Chinook and other Northwest cultures. He strongly argued for the equation of oral literature not with poetry or narrative but with drama, citing its laconic style rich in aesthetic and emotional complexity. Jacobs argued that literature provided social and psychological outlets otherwise repressed in public. In brief, characters and plots acted as projections of community concerns that could not otherwise be expressed without rancor.

Jacobs regarded narratives as a kind of theater, similar to the solo reading of a play, with all of the characters represented by distinctive accents, mannerisms, and pitches. Native people often have a particular fondness for cartoons because these images are most like their own stories, full of color and potential beyond the scope of ordinary life. Unfortunately this analogy is lost to most of a modern audience because cartoons are supposed to be for children.

Native stories lacked verbalized emotions because these were supplied by the audience, who knew the tales well from frequent retellings and so could personally emote with incidents and events.

One of the best collections of tribal narratives was provided by Clara Pearson of the Oregon Tillamook to Elizabeth Jacobs (1959) and edited by her husband, Melville Jacobs. Tillamook mythology explicitly recognized three temporal stages in the world. First, there was a precultural age noted for incompleteness, immaturity, incompetency, and great dangers. Next came a transitional age when Southwind made the world ready for the arrival of humans. Most recent was the modern cultural age filled with many traditions, a pluriverse rather than a universe of many tribes, traditions, and times.

Expanding the work of Jacobs was that of Dell Hymes (1981), a linguist and folklorist who also works with Oregon languages and tribes. While recognizing that a text is a dramatic play, he relied on linguistic features and tags to indicate an orderly patterning in acts and scenes in what he calls "measured verse." By skillfully blending a minute analysis of grammar with a concern with stylistics and performance features, Hymes has truly brought Native texts within the traditional purview of English literature.

The other accomplished scholar in this field, generally called ethnopoetics, is Dennis Tedlock, who worked at Zuni Pueblo and apprenticed as a Day Keeper among the Highland Maya. Tedlock has been particularly concerned with the presentation of texts in different print fonts to better convey a sense of performance details. As one convention, words printed in bigger type were those spoken in a louder voice. Gaps represented pauses and italics showed emphasis during a narrative performance.

By way of illustration, William Bright (1979) blended the contributions of Hymes and Tedlock for the presentation of a Karok text, told in English by Julia Starritt and called "Coyote Steal Fire."

In a recent collection of Athapaskan texts from the Dene Dhaa (Slavey), elders urged Patrick Moore and Angela Wheelock (1990: xxiv) to use a prose rather than a verse format, so as not to break up the thought flow by a series of poetic lines. The Dene Dhaa separate *eghasuli* "prayers," including *shin* "songs," from *wodih* "messages." Because they emphasize the message of the narrative, *wodih* seem to parallel English prose narratives, whereas *eghasuli* are structured more like chants and songs and depend on exact performance to achieve the desired goal.

A sweeping survey of the literatures of both North and South America was provided by the herculean labors of Claude Lévi-Strauss, a French anthropologist. In four volumes, collectively called mytho-logic (mythologique), he began with an account by Bororo of Brazil about a boy marooned in a tree while collecting bird eggs, and ended in the Pacific Northwest, over eight hundred texts later, with a discussion of the symbolism of naked initiates rescued from the forest.

Throughout, Lévi-Strauss was concerned with global human symbolism expressed as Nature/Culture in terms of modalities like accident/pattern or disorder/order. He insisted that no narrative detail was trivial and always expended great effort to explicate not only the big categories that were like trees and forests, but also smaller ones like twigs and leaves. His theory grew out of the recognition of general human patterns, particularly in the Americas. Scholars working in the Southwest often joke that his theory and practice are so interwoven that it is as though the Pueblos invented Lévi-Strauss to exemplify their culture.

Lévi-Strauss argued that all human creations were structured in terms of codes, variously concerned with biological, sociological, culinary, acoustic, astronomical, cosmological, and other modalities. Events were never random or haphazard. Fine minds had worked for centuries to hone and perfect these narratives.

For the first volume, the codes reflective of Nature/Culture were raw/cooked, and, then, in the other three volumes they were honey/tobacco ashes and sensory registers like sight/sound, and naked/clothed.

A radical feature of his "Structural Analysis" was an insistence that texts, to be understood, must be rethought in logical order because the intrigue and beauty of these narratives derived from mixing and matching codes and motifs. Such blendings were also ordered by the process of transformation.

In general, transformations progressively altered a set of relationships. Best known transformations include redundancies, where a relationship is expressed in several related ways; reversals, where the extremes or poles of a pair become switched; expansions, where an opposition was broadened to include more diverse elements; and neutralizations, where a firm contrast was made fuzzy or otherwise minimized.

As an example of these transformations, an opposition between land/water can be variously expressed. Thus, Hare might travel to a spring, lake, river, and sea during a tale to emphasize and expand on this distinction. Later, he might marry a mermaid, who came to live on land, thus reversing her normal associations. On another occasion, a frog appeared and, by virtue of being amphibious, blended the opposition of land/water.

For Lévi-Strauss, a single version of a text was never enough to provide understanding and analysis; rather, it was every and all versions of a text as well as the entire corpus of tribal and neighboring literatures that must be considered to arrive at an appreciation of structure.

Throughout, Lévi-Strauss argued that mythologies represented rational attempts to consider alternative cultural strategies, to intellectually solve paradoxes inherent between real and ideal behaviors, and to work out elaborate affirmations that the world is logical. He attributed to this "mytho-logic" the full canonical power that is reserved for "science" by the industrial nations.

More recently, Native oral literatures have become the subject of treatment by scholars in English and Comparative Literature. While some of these efforts suffer from a lack of cultural understanding, a failure to appreciate the profound differences involved, and a denial of the value of the original Native language texts, or a preference for those reduced to English, these writers have helped expand the appreciation and contributions of American oral traditions.

Chief among these scholars are Karl Kroeber and LaVonne Ruoff. Kroeber, the son of anthropologists, came to Indian literature after an established career in English literature. With a desire to make Native American literature more accessible, he urged greater attention to style and presentation than that displayed by scholars unskilled in the fine art of writing. As good literature, Native accounts should raise as many troubling problems as they answer, encouraging a diversity of interpretations and nuanced prose.

Another scholar calling greater attention to Native American literature is LaVonne Ruoff, through articles on the oral tradition as well as bibliographic aids and overviews.

Many Native authors have been published by Greenfield Review Press, whose editor, Joseph Bruchac, is himself a storyteller and writer. Tlingit tales and oratory have been superbly presented by Richard and Nora Marks Dauenhauer (1987), a poet and a Native speaker of Tlingit, respectively. Further, Lushootseed Salish books by Vi Hilbert (1985) combine careful translations, some in measured verse, with the insights of a cultural insider.

CLASSIC SOURCES

Significant early publications of stories in many Native American languages appeared in government and professional volumes, then later in a series founded by Franz Boas and his students. Thus, Columbia University Publications in Anthropology included important Northwest Coast text collections by Leo Frachtenberg from Coos and Lower Umpqua of coastal Oregon, by Manuel Andrade on Quileute for coastal Washington, and by Franz Boas from Kwakiutl and Bella Bella. This series is notable for close translations of Native language texts on the same or adjoining pages, but the texts lack abstracts and performance annotations.

Several Winnebago texts by Paul Radin were published in the Indiana University Publications in Anthropology and Linguistics.

Publications of the American Ethnological Society include separate volumes with story texts in Fox, Ojibwa, and Kickapoo by William Jones; Wishram by Edward Sapir; Tsimshian, Keresan, and Kwakiutl by Franz Boas; Maidu by Roland Dixon; Tena'a by John W. Chapman; Passamaquoddy by John Dyneley Prince; Menomini and Plains Cree by Leonard Bloomfield; Yuchi by Gunther Wagner; Dakota by Ella Deloria; Zuni by Ruth Bunzel; Caddoan by Gene Weltfish; Sahaptian by Melville Jacobs; Catawba by Frank Speck; and Nez Perce by Archie Phinney. Jones, Deloria, and Phinney were Native American scholars working in their own and related languages.

Memoirs of the American Anthropological Association includes a Jicarilla Apache tale of raiding, collected by Morris Opler (1938, # 52) and an overview of the career of Franz Boas (1959, # 89).

Bureau of American Ethnology Bulletins include extensive bibliographies for most language families compiled by James C. Pilling. Volume 40, collecting summary grammars of many Native languages, also includes texts for Maidu, Hupa, Fox, Tlingit, Haida, Chinook, Kwakiutl, Tsimshian, Eskimo, Dakota, Takelma, Coos, and Chuckchee. Separate volumes are devoted to materials from Chinook and Kathlamet Chinook and from Tsimshian by Franz Boas; Skidegate Haida and the Tlingit at Sitka and Wrangel by John Swanton; Alsea by Leo Frachtenberg; and some Nootkan and Quileute material by Frances Densmore. The series is characterized by generally close English translations from Native texts, along with short abstracts. There are no details on performance. Among the Annual Reports of the Bureau, the thirty-first includes the classic Boas (1916) study of Tsimshian and comparative North Pacific Coast mythology.

The University of Washington Publications in Anthropology contain fairly close English translations by Arthur Ballard for Puget

Sound Salish (Lushootseed) myths; by Erna Gunther for Klallam; by Leslie Spier and Edward Sapir for Wishram and Wasco; and by Melville Jacobs for Coos, Kalapuya, and Clackamas Chinook. These volumes generally include some performance and life history material on the narrators.

The Anthropological Papers of the American Museum of Natural History published mythology compiled by Boas from the Bella Coola and by Boas and George Hunt for the Kwakiutl. The John Swanton summary of Haida ethnography includes abstracts of his Skidegate, Masset, and Kaigani Haida texts.

The Memoirs of the American Folklore Society includes an uneven volume on Coast Salish by Thelma Adamson, one on the Bella Coola by Boas, and his final statement on the Kwakiutl. These memoirs are limited to English translations of varying quality, depending on the abilities of the collector. Abstracts are often included.

The many issues of the *Journal of American Folklore* are the best source for short collections of myths published in English. After about 1950, the authors have included more psychological, performance, stylistic, theoretical, and cultural information.

More recently, the journal of professional linguists, *The International Journal of American Linguistics,* published a Native American Text series. They are very informative, but not particularly readable. The two volumes each have three parts. The first one includes Mayan by Louanna Furbee-Losee; Otomi parables, folktales, and jokes by H. Russell Bernard and Jesus Salinas Pedraza; and Yuman by Margaret Langdon. The second volume has Caddoan edited by Douglas R. Parks, Northern California languages by Victor Golla and Shirley Silver, and a Northwest Coast collection edited by Barry Carlson in which all the texts tell the story of the theft of light.

Academic presses occasionally published scholarly editions. Noteworthy have been Chiricahua and Mescalero Apache Texts by Harry Hoijer through the University of Chicago Press, and Tunica texts by Mary R. Haas through the University of California Publications in Linguistics, which includes other text collections. Bella Coola stories were edited by Philip W. Davis and Ross Saunders and published at the British Columbia Provincial Museum in Victoria.

Other collections of authentic stories have been reissued by Bison Books of the University of Nebraska Press. The Alaska

Native Language Center in Fairbanks has issued stories in many native Alaskan languages. A good all-purpose collection is Erdoes and Ortiz (1984).

Various tribal governments are also collecting and publishing their own traditions, mostly for use in their classrooms. The most widely available of these efforts is the stories from the Pueblo of Zuni (1972) in New Mexico.

NOTES
▼▼▼▼▼▼

1. Versions of Earth Diver are widespread across the northern regions of America, Asia, and Europe. A printed version occurs in Coffin (1961: 10). The importance of song for expressing the rhythms of the universe was the subject of a lifetime of work by Frances Densmore. It was also emphasized in the work of Natalie Curtis and, in particular, *The American Rhythm: Studies and Reexpression of Amer-Indian Songs* by Mary Austin.

2. This Iroquois creation is well known. Most collections include it, as does Thompson (1929: 14). Fenton (1962) is the most careful treatment of this epic.

3. Other published versions include Coffin (1961: 15) from the neighboring Luisenyo and cultural discussions by Bean (1972). A native language version appears in Seiler (1970).

4. Sedna begins the entire collection of Thompson (1929).

5. The adventures of Hare or Rabbit throughout the East have also entered American literature through the work of Joel Chadler Harris. Versions of the epic were collected by William Jones and others for the Ojibwa.

6. Marriage to a star has a wide distribution across the Americas. Thompson (1929: 126, 128) includes two versions from Ojibwa and Arapaho.

7. Frog plays a significant role throughout the Americas. In the Northwest, Frogs were the prototypes for later species and the shamans of the animal world. Their associations with water and fire in the Basin and California are treated in Blackburn (1975). Chickadee and his mighty bow create an arrow chain in many Salishan stories (Mourning Dove 1990: 199).

8. The Caddo were an important confederacy of tribes located in Louisiana, Missouri, Texas, and Arkansas. They presently live in Oklahoma. A version of this appears in Lankford (1987: 126).

9. A wonderful telling of Coyote and the Swans by Charles Quintasket occurs in Mourning Dove (1990). The complexities of Coyote have been well discussed by Babcock (1975).

10. The Kootenay are a private and cautious people. This version of their origins was based on one collected by Franz Boas.

11. The story of lizard's hand also occurs in Thompson (1939: 38) from the Yokuts and is mentioned in the superb anthology by Gifford and Block (1990).

12. The epic of how Salmon was brought by Coyote up the Columbia River is still told among the people of the Colville Reservation. It has only appeared in professional reports, although other aspects of Colville literature were published by Mourning Dove (1990), a local native author.

13. Many such contests among the animals of different species are told across the Americas. Antelope and Deer shared life on the southern Plains.

14. Many Iktomi or Spider stories are still told among the Lakota. A version of this one occurs in accounts collected by James R. Walker (1983: 166), the agency physician at the Pine Ridge Agency from 1896–1914.

15. The story of Loon woman has a distinctive spread among tribes of northern California. Coffin (1961: 48) includes a Shasta version.

16. Versions of this story are still told to validate hereditary crests and dynastic houses. This version combines details from Tsimshian and Tlingit traditions.

17. All Southwestern Pueblos have stories about the valor and wisdom of turkeys. This version is based on one from Cochiti pueblo near Santa Fe, New Mexico.

18. Zuni and other Pueblo traditions are rich in accounts of the deeds of the War God twins who are believed to still live in the Sandia Mountains near Albuquerque. Blending versions from Zuni and Acoma, this story occurs midway in their career of ridding the earth of monsters.

19. The Cherokee story of Kanati and Selu is the basis for this version. A similar account occurs in Lankford (1987: 148).

20. The terror of Windigo continues today. This version is a composite of Cree and Ojibwa accounts.

21. The Cheyenne story of the Great Race is a tribal classic. John Stands in Timber and Margo Liberty (1967) summarize the tradition.

22. The Hidatsa are so well known because of the monumental work of Alfred Bowers (1965), who also recorded materials from Mandan (1950).

23. Jokes like these are widely known and told. The tradition of attributing life to all manner of things continues as one of their hallmarks. Versions of these jokes were told by Menomini and Lakota.

FURTHER READINGS
▼▼▼▼▼▼

Babcock, Barbara

    1975. A Tolerated Margin of Mess: The Trickster and His Tales Reconsidered. *Journal of the Folklore Institute* 9: 147–186. (Reprinted pp. 153–185 in *Critical Essays on Native American Literature.* Edited by Andrew Wiget, Boston: G. K. Hall, 1985.)

Ballard, Arthur C.

    1927. Some Tales of the Southern Puget Sound Salish. *University of Washington Publications in Anthropology* 2: 57–81.

    1929. Mythology of Southern Puget Sound. *University of Washington Publications in Anthropology* 3 (2): 31–150.

Bean, Lowell John

    1972. *Mukat's People: The Cahuilla Indians of Southern California.* Berkeley: University of California Press.

Blackburn, Thomas C.

    1975. *December's Child: A Book of Chumash Oral Narratives.* Berkeley: University of California Press.

Boas, Franz

    1894. Chinook Texts. *Bureau of American Ethnology, Bulletin* 20: 1–278.

    1896. The Growth of Indian Mythologies. *Journal of American Folklore* 9: 1–11.

    1898. The Mythology of the Bella Coola Indians. *Memoirs of the American Museum of Natural History* 2: 25–127.

    1901. Kathlamet Texts. *Bureau of American Ethnology, Bulletin* 26: 1–261.

    1902. Tsimshian Texts. *Bureau of American Ethnology, Bulletin* 27: 1–244.

    1905. Kwakiutl Texts. *Memoirs of the American Museum of Natural History* 5: 1–532.

    1906. Kwakiutl Texts, New Series. *Memoirs of the American Museum of Natural History* 1: 41–269.

    1910. Kwakiutl Tales. *Columbia University Contributions to Anthropology* 2: 1–495.

    1912. Tsimshian Texts, New Series. *Publications of the American Ethnological Society* 3: 65–284.

1914. Mythology and Folk-Tales of the North American Indians. *Journal of American Folklore* 27: 374–410.

1916. Tsimshian Mythology. *Bureau of American Ethnology, Annual Report* 31: 29–979.

1925. Keresan Texts. *Papers of the American Ethnological Society* 8.

1928. Bella Bella Texts. *Columbia University Contributions to Anthropology* 5: 1–291.

1929. Metaphorical Expressions in the Language of the Kwakiutl Indians. Reprinted 1949 as pp. 232–239 in *Race, Language, and Culture.* New York: The Macmillan Co.

1930. The Religion of the Kwakiutl Indians. *Columbia University Contributions to Anthropology,* 10: 1–284.

1932. Bella Bella Tales. *Memoirs of the American Folklore Society* 25.

1935. Kwakiutl Culture As Reflected In Mythology. *Memoirs of the American Folklore Society* 28: 1–190.

1935. Kwakiutl Tales, New Series. *Columbia University Contributions to Anthropology* 26 (1): 1–230.

1943. Kwakiutl Tales, New Series. *Columbia University Contributions to Anthropology* 26 (2): 1–228.

1949. *Race, Language, and Culture.* New York: The Macmillan Co.

Bowers, Alfred

1950. *Mandan Social and Ceremonial Organization.* University of Chicago Press.

1965. Hidatsa Social and Ceremonial Organization. *Bureau of American Ethnology, Bulletin* 194.

Bright, William

1957. A Karok Myth in Measured Verse. *Journal of California and Great Basin Anthropology* 1 (1): 117–123.

Bullchild, Percy

1985. *The Sun Came Down: The History of the World as My Blackfeet Elders Told It.* San Francisco: Harper and Row.

Chowning, Ann

1962. Raven Myths in Northwestern North America and Northeastern Asia. *Arctic Anthropology* 1 (1): 1–5.

Clark, Ella E.

1953. *Indian Legends of the Pacific Northwest.* Berkeley: University of California Press.

Coffin, Tristram, ed.

1961. *Indian Tales of North America. An Anthology for the Adult Reader.* Philadelphia: American Folklore Society 13.

Curtis, Natalie

1968. *The Indian's Book.* New York: Dover. [1907]

Dauenhauer, Nora Marks and Richard Dauenhauer

1987. *Haa Shuka, Our Ancestors: Tlingit Oral Narratives.* Volume 1. Seattle: University of Washington Press.

1990. *Haa Tuwunaagu Yis, for Healing Our Spirit. Tlingit Oratory.* Volume 2. Seattle: University of Washington Press.

de Laguna, Frederica

1972. *Under Mount Saint Elias.* Yakutat Tlingit. Washington, D.C.: Smithsonian Press.

Densmore, Frances

1939. Nootka and Quileute Music. *Bureau of American Ethnology, Bulletin* 124.

Dunn, John

1988. Aesthetic Properties of a Coast Tsimshian Text Fragment. Proceedings of the 23rd International Conference on Salish and Neighboring Languages, pp. 78–89.

Eastman, Charles and Elaine

1990. *Wigwam Evenings: Sioux Folktales Retold.* Lincoln: University of Nebraska Press. [1909]

Erdoes, Richard, and Alfonso Ortiz

1984. *American Indian Myths and Legends.* New York: Pantheon Books.

Fenton, William N.

1962. "This World, The World on Turtle's Back." *Journal of American Folklore* 75: 283–300. [Reprinted pp. 133–153 in *Critical Essays on Native American Literature.* Edited by Andrew Wiget, Boston: G. K. Hall, 1985.]

Garfield, Viola E.

1953. Contemporary Problems of Folklore Collecting and Study. *Anthropological Papers of the University of Alaska* 1 (2): 25–37.

Garfield, Viola E. and Paul S. Wingert

1966. *The Tsimshian and Their Arts.* Seattle: University of Washington Press.

Garfield, Viola E. and Linn A. Forrest

1961. *The Wolf and the Raven: Totem Poles of Southeastern Alaska.* Seattle: University of Washington Press.

Gifford, Edward W. and Gwendoline Harris Block

1990. *California Indian Nights.* Lincoln: University of Nebraska Press.

Hilbert, Vi

1985. *Haboo: Native American Stories from Puget Sound.* Seattle: University of Washington Press.

Hunt, George

1906. The Rival Chiefs, A Kwakiutl Story, in *Anthropological Papers Written in Honor of Franz Boas.* New York: G. E. Stechert and Co. pp. 108–136.

Hymes, Dell

1953. Two Wasco Motifs. *Journal of American Folklore* 66 (259): 69–70.

1965. Some North Pacific Coast Poems: A Problem in Anthropological Philology. *American Anthropologist* 67: 316–341.

1965. The Methods and Tasks of Anthropological Philology (Illustrated with Clackamas Chinook). *Romance Philology* 19 (2): 325–340.

1968. The "Wife" Who "Goes Out" Like A Man: A Reinterpretation of a Clackamas Chinook Myth. *Social Science Information* (Studies in Semiotics), 7 (3): 173–199.

1975. Breakthrough into Performance. pp. 11–74 in *Folklore and Communication.* Edited by Dan Ben-Amos and Kenneth Goldstein. The Hague.

1975. "Folklore's Nature and The Sun's Myth." *Journal of American Folklore* 88: 147–369.

1976. Louis Simpson's "The Deserted Boy." *Poetics* 5: 119–177.

1981. *"In Vain I Tried to Tell You." Essays in Native American Ethnopoetics.* Philadelphia: University of Pennsylvania Press.

1985. Language, Memory, and Selective Performance: Cultee's "Salmon Myth" as Twice Told to Boas. *Journal of American Folklore* 98 (390): 391–434.

Jacobs, Elizabeth Derr

1959. *Nehalem Tillamook Tales.* Eugene: *University of Oregon Studies in Anthropology* 5: 1–216.

Jacobs, Melville

1940. Coos Myth Texts. Seattle: *University of Washington Publications in Anthropology* 8.

1949. Kalapuya Texts. *University of Washington Publications in Anthropology* 11: 1–394.

1952. Psychological Inferences from a Chinook Myth. *Journal of American Folklore,* 65 (256): 121–137.

1959. A Few Observations on the World View of the Clackamas Chinook Indians. *Journal of American Folklore,* 68: 283–289.

1959. *The Content and Style of an Oral Literature: Clackamas Chinook Myths and Tales.* New York: Viking Fund Publications in Anthropology 26: 1–285.

1959. Folklore. In *Anthropology of Franz Boas. American Anthropologist* 61 (5), Part 2: 119–138.

1960. *The People Are Coming Soon: An Analysis of Clackamas Chinook Myths and Tales.* Seattle: University of Washington Press.

1962. The Fate of Indian Oral Literature in Oregon. *Northwest Review* 5: 90–99.

1966. A Look Ahead in Oral Literature Research. *Journal of American Folklore,* 79: 413–427.

1967. Our Knowledge of Pacific Northwest Indian Folklores. *Northwest Folklore* 2 (2): 14–21.

1972. Areal Spread of Indian Oral Genre Features in the Northwest States. *Journal of the Folklore Institute* 9 (1): 10–17.

Jones, William

1907. Fox Texts. *Publications of the American Ethnological Society* 1: 1–383.

1919. Ojibwa Texts. Edited by Truman Michaelson. *Publications of the American Ethnological Society* 7 (2).

Kinkade, Dale

1983. "Daughters of Fire": Narrative Verse Analysis of an Upper Chehalis Folktale. University of Oklahoma, Norman: *Papers in Anthropology* 24 (2): 267–278.

Laird, Carobeth

1975. *Encounter with an Angry God.* Banning, CA: Malki Museum Press

1976. *The Chemehuevis.* Banning, CA: Malki Museum Press

1984. *Mirror and Pattern: George Laird's World of Chemehuevi Mythology.* Banning, CA: Malki Museum Press

Lankford, George E., ed.

1987. *Native American Legends: Southeastern Legends.* Little Rock, AR: August House.

Lévi-Strauss, Claude

1967. The Story of Asdiwal, translated by Nicholas Mann, pp. 1–47 in *The Structural Study of Myth and Totemism.* Edited by Edmund Leach. London: ASA Monographs 5: 1–185.

1971. *L'Homme Nu.* Mythologiques 4. Paris: Plon.

1981. *The Naked Man: Introduction to The Science of Mythology,* Volume 4. Translated by John and Doreen Weightman. New York: Harper and Row.

MacDonald, George and John Cove

1987. *Tsimshian Narratives.* I: Trickster, Shamans and Heroes. II: Trade and Warfare. Canadian Museum of Civilization, Mercury Series, Directorate Paper 3.

McClellan, Catharine

1963. Wealth Woman and Frogs Among the Tagish Indians. *Anthropos* 58: 121–128.

1970. *The Girl Who Married the Bear.* Ottawa: National Museums of Canada, Publication in Ethnology, 2: 1–58.

Miller, Jay

1988. *Shamanic Odyssey: The Lushootseed Salish Journey to the Land of the Dead.* Menlo Park: Ballena Press.

Moore, Patrick, and Angela Wheelock, eds.

1990. *Wolverine Myths and Visions:* Dene Traditions from Northern Alberta. Compiled by the Dene Wodih Society. Lincoln: University of Nebraska Press.

Mourning Dove

1990. *Coyote Stories.* Lincoln: University of Nebraska Press.

Radin, Paul

1915. Literary Aspects of North American Mythology. Ottawa: Government Printing Bureau.

1923. The Winnebago Tribe. *Bureau of American Ethnology, Annual Report* 37 for 1915–16. pp. 35–560.

1945. *The Road of Life and Death: A Ritual Drama of the American Indians.* New York: Pantheon Books, Bollingen Series V.

1948. Winnebago Hero Cycles: A Study in Aboriginal Literature. *International Journal of American Linguistics* 14 (3).

1949. The Culture of the Winnebago: As Described by Themselves. *International Journal of American Linguistics* 15 (1).

1950. Winnebago Culture as Described by Themselves: The Origin Myth of the Medicine Rite. Three Versions along with The Historical Origins of the Medicine Rite. *Indiana University Publications in Anthropology and Linguistics, Memoir* 3.

1954. *The Evolution of an American Indian Prose Epic: A Comparative Study in Literature.* Bollingen Foundation, Special Publication 3.

1956. *The Evolution of an American Indian Prose Epic. A Study in Comparative Literature.* Bollingen Foundation, Special Publication 5.

Randall, Betty Uchitelle

1949. The Cinderella Theme in Northwest Coast Folklore. pp. 243–285 in *Indians of the Urban Northwest.* Edited by Marian Smith. New York: Columbia University Press, pp. 243–285.

Robinson, Harry

1989. *Write It on Your Heart: The Epic World of an Okanogan Story Teller.* Vancouver, BC: Talonbooks.

Rooth, Anna Birgitta

1957. The Creation Myths of the North American Indians. *Anthropos* 52: 497–508.

1962. *The Raven and the Carcass: An Investigation of a Motif in the Deluge Myth in Europe, Asia, and North America.* Helsinki: Academia Scientiarum Fennica. FF Communications 186.

Schutz, Noel W., Jr.

1975. The Study of Shawnee Myth in an Ethnographic and Ethnohistorical Perspective. Indiana University: Anthropology Ph.D. Dissertation.

Seiler, Hansjakob

1970. Cahuilla Texts with an Introduction. Bloomington: Indiana University, *Language Science Monographs* 6.

Spencer, Robert F.

1952. Native Myths and Modern Religion Among the Klamath Indians. *Journal of American Folklore* 65 (257): 217–226.

Stands In Timber, John, and Margot Liberty

1967. *Cheyenne Memories.* Lincoln: University of Nebraska Press.

Swanton, John R.

1905. Haida Texts and Myths. *Bureau of American Ethnology, Bulletin* 29.

1908. Haida Texts. *Memoirs of the American Museum of Natural History* 14: 273–812.

1909. Tlingit Myths and Texts. *Bureau of American Ethnology, Bulletin,* 39.

Tedlock, Dennis

1972. *Finding the Center: Narrative Poetry of the Zuni Indians.* New York: Dial Press.

Thompson, Stith

1929. *Tales of the North American Indians.* Cambridge: Harvard University Press.

Walker, James R.

1983. *Lakota Myth.* Edited by Elaine A. Jahner. Lincoln: University of Nebraska Press.

1980. *Lakota Belief and Ritual.* Edited by Raymond J. DeMallie and Elaine A. Jahner. Lincoln: University of Nebraska Press. [1990]

Waterman, Thomas T.

1914. The Explanatory Element in the Folktales of the North American Indians. *Journal of American Folklore* 27 (103): 1–54.

Zolbrod, Paul G.

1984. *Dine Bahane: The Navajo Creation Story.* Albuquerque: University of New Mexico Press.

Zuni People

1972. *The Zunis: Self-Portrayals.* Translated by Alvina Quam. New York: New American Library.

INDEX
▼▼▼▼▼

ABOUT THE AUTHOR
▼▼▼▼▼

Jay Miller has had a lifetime of involvement with the native peoples of the Americas. In addition to academic degrees from the University of New Mexico and Rutgers University, he has been instructed by elders from many tribes across North America. He has published dozens of articles in scientific journals and written or edited twenty books. Among these volumes are *Shamanic Odyssey: The Lushootseed Salish Journey to the Land of the Dead, Mourning Dove: A Salishan Autobiography,* and *The Tsimshian and Their Neighbors of the North Pacific Coast.*